PF

This book was written to be an encouragement

others who are facing the blackened face of the Grim Reaper sooner than expected. Having trekked in the Alps of Switzerland, Austria, Italy, France or Nepal annually for the last 21 years, I found myself experiencing air hunger for the first time during my last Swiss trek in Chamanna Coaz, an 8,500' snow and ice encased cliff-side mountain hut, tucked away in my bunk next to the open window as night fell. Crawling out of my sleeping bag and going outside gave me reassurance to see the distant sparkling lights of the closest village, 20 miles to the north, almost hidden in the forest. I wasn't sure if my air hunger was a physiological phenomenon with overtones of anxiety and exhaustion related to my cardiomyopathy or just exhaustion from the first days 5 hour trek to this isolated little hut. My cardiac ejection fraction, a measurement of the percentage of blood leaving the heart each time it contracts, had been stable over the last 15 years in the low 30's due to cardiomyopathy, while the normal range is 50-75. However, with this persistent air hunger was a new phenomenon, I suspected that the degree of my exhaustion was the result of an irreversible reduction of cardiac function, in spite of a normal pulse rate and rhythm. With heavy snow falling the last few miles of our trek, it now embraced the hut and the rocky trail was totally obliterated. It would be 36 hours until the trail would be sufficiently exposed to safely descend the narrow rocky cliff side and arrive to the safety of the forest, if there weren't any additional storms. During that next day of waiting out the storm for the trail to be exposed, a supply helicopter landed on the small primitive wooden helicopter pad adjacent to the hut, to quickly unload and leave within minutes. My ego would prevent me from investigating hitching a lift.

The diminished cardiac function was later confirmed with the ejection fraction having dropped to between 16 and 19. The prognosis based upon this degree of trajectory decline is consistent with conditions incompatible with life, and demise within a few months. As a result of this uncertain and dire prognosis, I decided to document my spiritual thoughts which has taken these 12 months, grateful to the grace of God to still be here.

I have been blessed the last 21 years with the opportunity to explore the alpine trails. The 4 to 6 week duration treks were different every year but always included huts with exceptionally superb views and gracious hospitality. There were many adventure-filled treks; the first 13 years alone, and the last 8 with my wonderful son, Robert. In addition to my alpine adventures, I am also thankful for experiences in Hawaii, California and Mexico in Top Cat, my Australian built 24' cabin cruiser. Exploration of Espiritu Santo, an island north of La Paz, the fishing grounds of the Cape. Being buzzed by Mexican helicopters suspicious I'm smuggling drugs across the Sea of Cortez to Southern Baja. The wonderful memories are still present as if yesterday of sleeping on the deck in the Cabo marina peacefully drifting off to nightly cantina music reflecting across the calm bay waters. Saving the lives of 3 Americans in their disabled cruiser 20 miles south of Cabo San Lucas during a storm. They would have otherwise been an unfortunate statistic, subject to the wishes of the winds and the strong southern flow of the California current blending with the Northern Equatorial current to the direction of the Philippines. It was fortunate that I recognized their frantic universal distress signals while returning from trolling in the vicinity. Yes, I must admit at first I thought they were all just waving an over-enthusiastic greeting.

Looking back at my life, I compare the variety of trekking adventures to those of metaphorical spiritual events. At times in our daily walk, we are trekking with little progress in knee-deep snow. A sudden life-threatening avalanche, no fault of our own overtakes us, a near miss. The challenge of overflowing rivers to be crossed. Vanished trails from washouts. Physical difficulty from heavy rain to the goal of a destination; winds, snow and hail obliterate the path. Narrow unstable trails damaged by the elements along rocky high cliffs. Steep drop offs. The rapid overtaking of afternoon mountain storm fronts with the sudden enormous flash of lightning bolts directly above and thunder pounding the entire sky in the same moment. Glacier crossings that developed life-swallowing crevices with unstable surface edges since the last trek to the area. Also unique to glacier crossings are the sudden threatening bowel sounds of rivers far beneath the surface eroding massive chunks of ice like the roar of an alpha lion beneath you. Sudden fear immediately fills the mind with the thought of a massive ice implosion drawing you to unknown depths. Immense boulder fields that hide the trail, a result of winter storms and avalanches and the risk of a new dislodgement while attempting to find an uncharted way. Precipitation or clouds so thick as to hide the trail, and one loses direction as dark approaches with the thought of spending the night in the safety of a "brown bear" cave. Of course there is always the temptation to deviate from the trail to take what appears to be an obvious shortcut - an easier way.

99% of the time this is a disastrous choice and will result in encountering danger and the backtracking of one's steps, compromising time and energy. Spiritual experiences in one's daily life can be related metaphorically to these trail experiences. Stay on the right trail, plan your work and work your plan, and always be ready for the unexpected. Prepare in advance for all possible encounters and always have a backup plan.

I find reassurance to daily look at my life from the vantage of Biblical apologetics that prove the presence of the God of the cosmos and the indwelling Holy Spirit as my promised eternal companion.

In medical and surgical study, knowledge, wisdom and technical skills are achieved only as a result of the repetitious, over and over review from all possible diagnostic and surgical case presentations, with the goal to arrive at the most accurate and successful conclusion. So it is with the construction of this text, to emphasize repetition to reinforce and ingrain thought for confidence and motivation.

To write this expanded and revised Second Edition is the result of encouragement from many sources; readers in Canada, Toronto to Vancouver, USA, Nepal, India and Africa. I received a series of photographs and brief biographies of disciples from the "Billy Graham" of Northern India and Nepal, all holding my book. I became acquainted with this charismatic gentleman in past years on mission trips to remote Himalayan villages in the Langtang and Annapurna regions, including always a number of his disciples who share in reaching the villagers with the gospel in song and testimony. In September, he is also including my book on a trip to Bhutan where he will be teaching pastors. Unfortunately due to the persecution of Christians, I cannot risk publishing the names of these beautiful young people, though they would love to share their individual stories, challenging to our laid back lifestyle of easy faith. I have included ten with permission to in this text. Since last September, the predominantly Hindu government in Nepal passed laws making it a crime to proselytize Christianity.

In Northern India, the RSS, a Hindu militant branch supported by the current government, is savagely persecuting Christians. Our heartfelt prayers are with these disciples who put their lives on the line facing persecution as well as total rejection and ostracism from family. One fellow I know who later became a successful pastor in a 14,000' elevation Himalayan village, was forced to live for a year in an adjacent yak quarters, sleeping with the animals, no longer permitted in the family house. It is not unusual for these motivated disciples to have established several home churches. In spite of persecution, Christianity numbers are growing with gatherings in home churches sprouting up as seedlings all over Nepal. Each time I fly into Kathmandu, I feel an undeniable evil spiritual oppression, reinforced when visiting the cultic rituals of burning the dead at the Bagmati river edge in the center of Kathmandu with relatives gathered. The embers later to be shoveled into the Bagmati river, considered sacred by both Hindus and Buddhists. The area filled with cultic Hindu worshipers, pundits and priests.

The African connection is with AFNET, a well organized mission organization specializing in training pastors and lay leaders in sub-equatorial countries as well as maintaining orphanages. The dominant regional issues they face are the historical contamination of animism to the Christian doctrine, voodoo and most recently the money influence behind Islam. I have known the founder of AFNET and his family for over 40 years with a close personal friendship. At

5

the time of writing this, Johan is traveling 4,000 miles round trip by van from South Africa to multiple areas in Zambia with leadership training materials and water purifiers for orphanages, in addition to speaking engagements.

A difficult road trip filled with multiple physical and political hazards and dangers including anticipated roadblocks requiring bribes, though the road does pass by the magnificent Victoria falls on the border of Zimbabwe and Zambia.

Please read and reread this revised edition as I do, with pause, ponder, rumination, personal reflection, application, transformation in the mind and most of all enjoy.

Ralph A. Kemp, M.D., F.A.C.O.G.
Diplomate American Board of Obstetrics and Gynecology, September 2018

DEDICATED DISCIPLES OF NORTHERN INDIA AND NEPAL

OMDEN LEPCHA....
PASTORING FIVE CHURCHES
AND ACTIVE IN TRAINING
PASTORS IN INDIA, NEPAL
AND BHUTAN.

BINOD KATWAL...
FROM NEPAL.
PASTORING A CHURCH
THAT HE
IS PASTORING.

BIGYAN SHRESTHA ...
FROM NEPAL, WORKING
IN THE HIMALAYAN REGION
AS A CHURCH PLANTER
AND PASTOR.

SALOMIE LEPCHA...
A STRONG PROVEN DISCIPLE
FROM INDIA.
AFTER GRADUATION SHE
JOINED CAMPUS CRUSADE
FOR CHRIST AND
NOW SERVING GOD IN
THE STATE OF SIKKIM

KUMAR RAI...
FROM THE STATE OF
MANIPUR IN INDIA.
GRADUATED WITH A MASTER
OF DIVINITY FROM
A SEMINARY IN THE PHILIPPINES.
NOW SERVING WITH
THE EVANGELICAL TEAM
IN INDIA.

YUSUF PRADHAN...
YOUTH LEADER FOR
BETHEL UNITED YOUTH
FELLOWSHIP. COMES FROM
A VERY FAITHFUL CHRISTIAN
FAMILY. HE HAS POTENTIAL
TO BE A GREAT LEADER
IN THE FUTURE.

CHATRA SUBBA ...
CAME TO THE LORD WHILE
IN COLLEGE..
FROM A NON CHRISTIAN FAMILY
BACKGROUND ...
IS STILL BEING PERSECUTED BY HIS
FAMILY FOR HIS FAITH IN CHRIST.
JUST THIS MONTH JOINED CAMPUS
CRUSADE FOR CHRIST AND IS
GOING TO SERVE GOD IN THE STATE
OF ARUNACHAL PRADESH. A VERY
DIFFICULT PLACE TO BE.

DINU THAPA,
THIS YOUNG MAN HAS
BEEN EXPELLED
FROM HIS VILLAGE,
TOLD THAT HE IS DEAD
TO THE FAMILY.
HE ALSO ENJOYED
READING "THE LORD
IS MY SHEPHERD."

SONU THAKUR...
COMES FROM A HINDU FAMILY
TOTALLY AGAINST HIS
CHRISTIAN FAITH.
HE IS BEING THREATENED BY
FAMILY AND COMMUNITY TO
EXCOMMUNICATE HIM.
THIS HAS SERIOUS
CONSEQUENCES IN SOUTH ASIA.
HE REMAINS STRONG IN HIS
CHRISTIAN FAITH.

BHAKTI GHALE...
FROM INDIA, REJECTED
BY HER NON-CHRISTIAN FAMILY.
SHE IS THE ONLY BELIEVER
IN HER FAMILY.
SUBJECTED TO PERSECUTION
AND DENIED FAMILY
RECOGNITION.
JOINED CAMPUS CRUSADE
FOR CHRIST AFTER GRADUATION
AND SERVING GOD IN
THE STATE OF SIKKIM.

DEDICATED DISCIPLES OF SOUTH AFRICA AND ZAMBIA

KANIKA BIBLE COLLEGE OF ZAMBIA

JOHN MULENGE,
A DEVOTED YOUNG MAN,
WITH GREAT POTENTIAL
FOR THE LORD.
STUDYING FOR THE
MINISTRY AT THE
KANIKI BIBLE
COLLEGE IN ZAMBIA.

KASUBA CHANDA! THE VERY FIRST ORPHAN JOHAN TOOK INTO THE ZAMBIA ORPHAN PROGRAM. HE JUST GRADUATED IN JUNE WITH A BACHELOR'S DEGREE IN MINISTRY. JOHAN RAISED THE FUNDS TO SEND HIM TO UNIVERSITY, AND WE ARE SO PLEASED AT HOW WELL HE DID. NOW DOING HIS ONE YEAR INTERNSHIP UNDER THE MENTORING PROGRAM BEFORE BEING SENT OUT AS A NEW CHURCH PLANTER TO A REMOTE VILLAGE AREA. HE'S TURNING INTO A GREAT EVANGELIST.

1.

BISHOP MUMBA IS
JOHAN'S ZAMBIA NATIONAL
COORDINATOR, OVERSEEING
THE BIBLE SCHOOL
PROGRAMS AS WELL AS
OVERSEER FOR THE ZAMBIA
ORPHAN WORK.
JOHAN MET HIM AS A YOUNG
STUDENT IN BIBLE SCHOOL
IN 1984 AND HAS BEEN A
PRIMARY MENTOR TO HIM SINCE!
HE IS PART OF JOHAN'S
PERMANENT TEAM.

PASTOR ESAU MUWOWO
ESAU GRADUATED FROM THE
BIBLE SCHOOL PROGRAM
LAST YEAR. HE WAS A GOOD
STUDENT, VERY SERIOUS, AND
SMART. SO HE IS NOW SERVING
AS THE FACILITATOR OFFICER
AT THE NEWEST EXTENSION
BIBLE SCHOOL IN NDOLA,
ZAMBIE. HE HAS 25 LEADERS
ENROLLED IN THAT 2 YEAR
PROGRAM. HE CAME THROUGH
TO ATTEND THE REGIONAL
MEETING IN MANSA. AN ALL
DAY BUS RIDE. GOOD YOUNG
MAN WITH 5 CHILDREN.

TOM MUSELEPETE,
RETIRED SCHOOL PRINCIPAL,
AND NOW HEAD ELDER
AND VOLUNTEER PRINCIPLE
OF THE ORPHAN CENTER
IN MANSA, ZAMBIA.

CORNELIUS MAPALO
IS ONE OF THE ORIGINAL
ORPHANS WHO IS JUST
ABOUT TO COMPLETE
BIBLE COLLEGE AND
BE SENT OUT AS A
CHURCH PLANTER.

"OUR ETERNAL CHOICE"

14

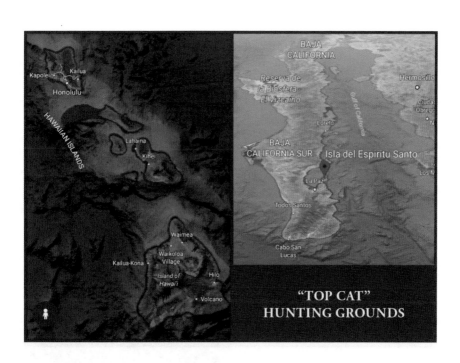

"TOP CAT"
HUNTING GROUNDS

"TOP CAT" HAS PROVEN
HERSELF IN 15' SWELLS
MOLOKAI CHANNEL,
18' OUTRIGGERS
NOT PICTURED

"GORNER GLACIER, 2ND LONGEST GLACIER IN THE ALPS"

BERGHAUS
MATTERHORN &
HÖRNLI - HÜTTE
3260 MüM
Lager u. Doppelzimmer

UNNERVING ROARS FROM DEEP BENEATH THE
SURFACE WITH IMAGES OF BEING SWALLOWED
INTO A COLLAPSING CREVICE IMPLOSION"

"3000 CLIMBERS
ATTEMPT TO REACH
THE 14,692' SUMMIT
PER YEAR WITH
AN AVERAGE OF
3-4 FATALITIES"

"DRONE
VIEW FROM
MATTERHORN
SUMMIT"

This text is designed to be a thoughtful, rich and logical paradigm for daily thought, reassurance and strengthening of one's confidence:

1. Jesus as the creator and God of the cosmos and having a personal relationship with him.
2. The urgency to address the eternal significance of the corruption that dominates our souls.
3. The importance of our total surrender to the Lordship of Christ and a new birth arising in our souls.
4. Strengthen Biblical neural pathways with meditation, rumination and memory to replace the subversive, subconscious/unconscious dominance that currently influences our thoughts and behavior.
5. Live at all times in the awareness of the presence of the Holy Spirit for the new redirection of our thoughts and behavior pleasing to God. Romans 12:1-2.

Ezekiel 36:24-27, "For I will take you out of the nations; I will gather you from all the countries and bring you back into your own land. I will sprinkle clean water on you and you will be clean; I will cleanse you from all your impurities and from all your idols. I will give you a new heart and put a new spirit in you; I will remove from you your heart of stone and give you a heart of flesh. I will put my spirit in you and move you to follow my decrees and be careful to keep my laws." 1st Peter 1:23-25, "For you have been born again, not of seed which is perishable but imperishable, that is, through the living and abiding word of God." "All flesh is like grass. And all its glory like the flower grass. The grass withers, and the flower falls off, but the word of the Lord abides forever." Isaiah 40:6-8, 1st Peter 1:24-25.

God designed the universe and all life from atoms, and gave humans a spirit to communicate. We are different from all other creatures. My atoms will be recycled, but my spirit will be either in hell or heaven dependent upon my heartfelt trust in the gospel of Jesus as Lord, following a metamorphosis from self to a new birth of conversion and regeneration from the seed of belief in Jesus Christ as Lord. Without Gospel medicine; the blood of Christ applied to us personally, we will die in bondage attached to a decaying corpse of sin. Sin is a hereditary disease that increases with age. Hades is the destination of this lost unrepentant sinner. Wake up before it's too late, if you are on your way to hell.

Every person knows in his heart with whom he is bonded. Self with the barnacles of sin and despair or a Christ surrender with a new hull. As soon as we receive a wakeup call to our unrepentant soul and realize our ultimate destination, it should draw us closer to belief in Jesus, the gospel and His love. A heartfelt belief is not only the solution to troubled thoughts of our final destination but as a result of surrender to Christ, our physiology is influenced. Brain hormones are secreted when meditating on God's love; dopamine, serotonin and oxytocin. All levels are elevated as a result when love is a dominant thought in our brains. These neurotransmitters target neurons and synapses that contribute to the level of our well-being for both physiological and psychological health. Why would you want to live your remaining short life with marginalized physical and mental health when you possess the secret provided by our maker for living on the cutting edge? Our dominant thoughts should be based upon apologetics, that through logic and reason we verify God's love for us, his presence and our heartfelt belief and trust in the gospel. We are made from space dust, atoms, the result of the origin of the universe. None are lost, all are recycled. You may currently have the atoms from a dinosaur of 200 million years past or possibly from the mud between his toes.

Do I live daily from the lower brainstem; "sensory feelings" or belief? It's not what happens to me but what happens in me that should determine my response. What we believe is more important than transitory feelings from our sensory receptors. Yes, God made us from space dust, but gave us a spirit and soul and complex cognitive ability that allows us to live by belief if we so choose. The love of God is the cross and the "precious" blood of Jesus. 1st. Peter 1:18-19. When we acknowledge the love of God, think on the cross and of the total gospel. God's love was the sacrifice of his Son, love that we can understand on a human level. The love God offers for mankind was demonstrated at the crucifixion of Jesus at Calvary. A sacrificial love so triumphant that through agony and death all past, present and future sin was, and is voided for those who believe and trust in Jesus. Micah 7:18-19, "Who is a God like thee, who pardons iniquity and passes over the rebellious act of the remnant of His possession? He does not retain His anger forever, because He delights in unchanging love. He will have compassion on us; He will tread our inequities under foot. Yes, Thou wilt cast all their sins into the depths of the sea." Psalm 103:12-13, "As far as the east is from the west, so far has He removed our transgressions from us. Just as a father has compassion on his children, so the Lord has compassion on those who fear Him." At the moment of His death, the impenetrable temple veil representing man's sin barrier to God was torn open. All sins were forgiven then and now for all believers. Believers now have access to the Holy of Holies (God) through their surrender to Jesus as Lord. With sin and guilt saturated souls now flushed clean following belief and repentance, Jesus stands at the door of your heart knocking. One must open the door to experience the fullness of his personal love, the Holy Spirit. Jesus is the only person upon whose love you can eternally depend. Do I live in bondage to self defeat and self degradation or by belief in God's love and forgiveness? Yes, I am blessed with an undeserved plethora of God's grace, every day. My goal is to share the how, why and urgency to become right with God now before our last breath. Do we have a burden in our hearts for lost souls who have hardened hearts to the message of the gospel and unaware of their ultimate fate?

Are you resigned to being a random choice, the end result being a fortuitous conception in a universe ruled by chance? I am the result of one sperm out of 200 million possibilities at one event, roughly the 4th of July 1935. I am not a random event. On God's word, I believe my life and future was planned in advance. Psalm 139:14-16, "I will give thanks to Thee, for I am fearfully and wonderfully made; wonderful are Thy works, and my soul knows it well. My frame was not hidden from Thee, when I was made in secret, and skillfully wrought in the depths of the earth. Thine eyes have seen my unformed substance; and in Thy book they were all written, the days that were ordained for me, when as yet there was not one of them." Ralph is a clay pot with a treasure, if I contain a heartfelt belief in the gospel. Always remember Job, his questions, faith and hopes were eventually fulfilled. God is omnipresent, even if you feel his presence or not. Be an overcomer. "He chose us in him before the creation of the world to be holy and blameless in his sight."Ephesians 1:4. We can believe God's omnipresence yet transcendence with full assurance as did Job.

24

Billions of souls have believed this to be their guiding truth since Job of 4000 years ago, and is the golden thread running the entire length from Genesis through Revelation on which we can rest our faith.

To live as an overcomer one must not be controlled by selfish desires, therefore, as instructed, carry your cross, your sinful inclinations to be crucified, and surrender to the Lordship of Christ. Luke 9:23, Romans 6:4-7. Everything is dependent upon the surrender of self to the lordship of Christ. Starts with belief, acknowledging the acceptance of God's love and the implantation of the seed of belief in the historical reality of Jesus and truth of the Gospel into our corrupt soul for metamorphosis and rebirth. Our motivation is the realization of the final destiny of a corrupt unrepentant soul. No other life form can respond to God's love with control of behavior and thought dominated by the cerebral cortex over the lower brainstem. All designed by God, an advance of evolution for a divine personal spiritual fellowship with the God of the cosmos through the Holy Spirit. If I do not respond to God's unconditional love for a spiritual rebirth than I will remain spiritually dead. I must awaken to the reality that we are spiritual beings who indwell this fallible body for only a short time and face two options at death. Satan attempts to mask and hide this fact through self and worldly dominance. The consistent employment of wisdom, based upon the influence of the Holy Spirit should be our ultimate goal following our awakening. Holiness is not in our effort to become right with God but we will naturally want to be holy as a result of our new relationship as loved adopted sons and daughters. Another way to explain this perspective; we don't sin to gain God or from fear of God, rather we don't sin because we know God.

Wisdom is knowing what's right and doing it. Do not be controlled or influenced by self, Satan, nor by worldly fashions of the day to dominate or control our thinking. Human nature is influenced by choice; self, Satan or world influence. To overcome, we must plug our heartfelt belief and trust in Jesus into the awaiting socket of God's love, the antidote to fear, hopelessness, guilt, and enjoy the confidence and presence of God's unconditional love. The magnitude of this love to replace our negative mental preoccupations has been described as the overwhelming love and desire that a pregnant women experiences upon feeling the first movements of her fetus. This is the love from God that is available to us to enjoy every day if we live by belief and remove self as our god. Psalm 103:8, "The Lord is compassionate and gracious, slow to anger, and abounding in love." The word for compassionate in Hebrew is a derivative of "womb," thus attempting to describe this love for us as a mother's love and passion for her new gift of life, awareness from the first movements detected in her womb. As we live in the confidence of God's love, we should be motivated to the expectations that we know God desires. To please him, our thought paradigm is best expressed by the Beatitudes. To effect a real change, we must take aim at our corrupt souls as the bullseye for change. We cannot express Jesus is Lord without full surrender to his Lordship. This is best revealed by our ethos and behavior. 1st John 3:18. Our poisoned, corrupt soul prior to conversion drags with ignorance and effort our heavy baggage of sin in total darkness prior to seeing light. Matthew 4:16, Isaiah 9:2, "The people who were sitting in the darkness saw a great light, and those who were sitting in the land of the shadow of death, upon them a light dawned."

If I have a ruler or king, then he should be in my thoughts daily and how to please him. If God rules over the universe, why should he not rule over me? What one fears controls your life. The antidote is God's love, the Holy Spirit, for a life free of fear and full of thanksgiving. Do I want my life controlled by fear or God's love? Unfortunately we tend to live our lives with spiritual mediocrity, rather we should be living daily, recharged from above, as Paul prays, summarized from Ephesians 3:16-21, "...strengthened with power through His Spirit in the inner man...Christ may dwell in your hearts through faith...rooted and grounded in love...comprehend the breadth and length and height and depth...to know the love of Christ which surpasses knowledge...filled up to all the fullness of God...according to the power that works within us...to all generations forever and forever." The truth and metaphor that the "Lord is my Shepherd" is very appropriate and understandable. The Shepherd knows each of us, indwells us, grafted to Him to bare fruit, we see Him, hear Him and feel His touch. As we enjoy His blessed company, this knowledge, protection and intimacy is the most precious of all relationships. For three thousand years, the 23rd. Psalm has provided billions of people with a beauty of imagery, confidence, promise and hope.

Satan has had varying degrees of success attempting to distort and scramble God's message to every generation throughout history. There is only one living being who has totally and effectively defeated Satan with complete success and that is Christ. He defeated Satan at the cross with his death and resurrection. That should be where we left our sins and sorrows, now to enjoy the resurrection of our new life in Christ. If the Holy Spirit was absent in the world today can you imagine the extent of despair, turmoil, grief and evil? Is it not smart to

27

be with the ultimate winner? This must be decided before our last breath, a decision of eternal consequence. Romans 6:23, "For the wages of sin is death, but the gift of God is eternal life in Christ Jesus our Lord."

100% of our atoms are from the origin of the universe, space dust. Chaos converted to order by God. Include this in your apologetic statement. Our atoms are recycled, our spirits live on, either in hell or heaven following physical death. What do you believe? I believe in the God of love. Start with apologetics, which offers proof of validity of the gospel. God created the cosmos and life, with man given a sense of eternity in his heart and an eternal soul. We experience heartfelt love following a conversion to a new birth based on belief.

I believe that with a too shallow, superficial belief, most people do not experience the love of God in their lives. Simply limited to a conversational belief, but not a heartfelt belief. Not plugged into the socket of belief and God's love. A cosmetic religiosity with no remittance of sins. Without the assurance of God's love, one cannot have the assurance of the Holy Spirit or of eternal life. The sovereignty of God must rule our thoughts. Apologetics are so important to provide evidence of his presence at **this** moment and the truth of the equality of the trinity. There is no hiding from the omnipresence of God. Following conversion, it is absolute for us to visualize daily the indwelling presence of the Holy Spirit, my intermediary to God.

Ephesians 2:10,"For we are His workmanship, created in Christ Jesus for good works, which God prepared beforehand, that we should walk in them." If I approach each new day from God's perspective, these good works will be revealed, thus the Christian life will be a daily adventure of discovery and satisfaction.

Pray throughout the day with thanksgiving, Philippians 4:4-7. Experiencing his presence we can express a heartfelt thankfulness. Is my love too shallow? I should glow with a halo of thankfulness, immediately identified by my ethos, equal to the immediate effervescence upon opening a fermenting cider. 1st Peter 3:15, "but sanctify Christ as Lord in your heart, always be ready to make a defense to everyone who asks you to give an account for the hope that is in you, yet with gentleness and reverence." I can only reflect this if truly grateful for a deep feeling of thankfulness for God's grace and the indwelling Holy Spirit. Thanksgiving throughout the day displaces worry and anxiety, and should be my trademark. This is an example of replacement therapy as will be discussed later in detail. To be an overcomer have a strong apologetic statement with belief and trust in your heart as a gift from God, and plug into the awaiting God's love. This will set aside Christ in our heart as Jesus is Lord and death to self, resulting in eternal hope. One must be an overcomer to self, Satan and the world. My hope and God's love should be so evident that people question our affect of confidence.

How can I show people an authentic abounding hope? The answer is a personal ethos of confidence and authentic encouragement to others. Short-term shallow hope and encouragement can be achieved as a result of personal accomplishments, from people, pills, psychiatrists, however the only long term source of encouragement and hope of proven permanency is that found in Romans 15:13, from total surrender and trust in Christ, "May the God of hope **fill** you with **all** joy and peace in trusting him, that you will **abound in hope** through the power of the Holy Spirit." How can we enjoy this presence of lasting hope and encouragement? The answer is obvious, only through a spiritual epiphany with surrender to the God of creation and an indwelling relationship with the Holy Spirit that by faith lives within you, as if grafted to the Holy Spirit identified with a rebirth of the soul. Encouragement is such an important ingredient and indicator of psychological health of our soul, an endowment through the power of the Holy Spirit and should be in our hearts to share. Inward spiritual confidence is expressed outwardly by our joy. The source of my inward spiritual confidence is equal to the thoughts and anticipation of a fisherman patiently waiting with his hook in the water for extended periods of time in the anticipation of the joys of a catch. So God has waited for me, months and years for his delight in forgiving me through his grace, mercy and compassion with the love of an expectant mother, a result of my faith. God's forgiveness, grace and mercy makes His own heart glad. Christ came to reconcile sinners to God. His ministry was called "the pleasure of the Lord". Isaiah 53:10. "and it gave him great pleasure". Ephesians 1: 3-10. Ephesians 2:5-7, "even when we were dead in our transgressions, made us alive together with Christ (by grace you have been saved), and raised us up with Him, and seated us with Him in the heavenly places, in Christ Jesus, in order that in the ages to come He might show the surpassing riches of His grace in kindness toward us in Christ Jesus." We will be on display in his living celestial museum as treasures from a corrupt world, prizes of his grace. To be further encouraged, Philippians 3:20-21,"For our citizenship is in heaven, from which also we eagerly wait for a Savior, the Lord Jesus Christ; who will transform the body of our humble state into conformity with the body of His glory...."

With a valid conversion to the Lordship of Christ, one must experience the desire to determine thinking based upon the

30

Beatitudes, taught during the Sermon on the Mount. Matthew 5:3-11. This is the path to "restoration of the soul." Psalm 23:3. Express always an attitude of thanksgiving, genuine love for life, reflecting on God's love for you. This habit of thought has been demonstrated to increase production of our neurotransmitter hormones resulting in a positive influence to physiological and psychological health. When our minds are focused on love, dopamine, serotonin and oxytocin are all elevated. With anxiety and depression these hormone blood levels are depressed. With happiness, only serotonin is elevated. Therefore when the cerebral cortex facilitates an awareness of God's love, the result is a proven stimulus for the elevation of these three critical hormones. Let's remind ourselves daily of this beneficial God given cause and effect mechanism. The best source of a psychological feeling of well being is when you ponder on the love someone has for you.

The message of Jesus is not only the proclamation of salvation but the announcement of judgment. Do I want to meet Jesus as savior or judge? We make the choice. An urgent message for us while we are still alive, yet spiritually dead, truly an urgent crisis. As sure as sunrise and sunset, judgment is on the horizon. What is the current health status of your soul? Would God consider you spiritually dead, a slave to self?

Thanksgiving is a choice, a constant state of being thankful in all things. It dominates over selfishness and worry. Not just for material blessings but thankfulness for the presence of God now and daily. Thankfulness should rest on the foundation of Jesus is Lord for full expression and enjoyment. Unfortunately, our proclivity is to be preoccupied with worry and anxiety. Our evolutionary features and gifts have progressed beyond this to a new dimension, a God

31

receptiveness, with the ultimate goal to "Glorify God and enjoy him forever," motivated to reach the spiritual expectations and desires of the one who unconditionally loves us.

In our youth, dominated by the flesh, we think we know and will know everything. In old age, we realize we know nothing.

Our beliefs should be more important to determine our thoughts and behavior than our feelings. A normal trajectory to birth a Christian faith is progressing from the epiphany of general and specific revelation apologetics to belief, followed by plugging into the socket of God's awaiting love of Revelation 3:20. My thought of God's love for me is not fabricated but dependent upon God's word, his resurrection, logic and the historical evidence of Christ.

Our desire to follow the Beatitudes is an attempt to heal and restore our corrupt soul. We must be an overcomer if we desire to follow Jesus as Lord. I want my dominant thought life to progresses from the 1st through the 8th Beatitude, resulting in an intravenous Beatitude infusion to replace a rotten soul. From misery to happy realignment with Jesus is our goal. Matthew 5:3-10. The Beatitudes begin with the acknowledgment of our need and anticipation for a restored soul, "Blessed are the poor in spirit, for theirs is the kingdom of heaven." The admission of a diseased and uninformed soul, yet with potential. "Blessed" is translated as "happy". Only with a restored, Christ centered soul can we express the Beatitudes as a lifestyle.

APPENZELL TREK

A LOVELY EASY TREK IN APPENZELL. TRAIN AND 5 MINUTE BUS TO BRULISAU AND SEILBAHN TO HOHER KASTEN 5,800'. ENJOYING VIEWS, EAST TO AUSTRIA, SOUTHEAST TO LICHTENSTEIN, VIEWING THE ORIGIN OF THE RHINE RIVER AS IT EMPTIES INTO THE BODENSEE TO THE NORTH. LOVELY VIEWS SOUTH AND WEST INTO SWITZERLAND. 1 1/2 HOUR TRAIL WALK TO BERGGASTHAUS STAUBERN. FOLLOWING DAY, TREK SOUTH ABOVE SAMTISERSEE ON A HIGH TRAIL, DESCENDING TO CHARMING BERGGASTHAUS BOLLENWEES ON THE NORTH EDGE OF THE PICTURESQUE FALENSEE. PEACEFUL AND QUIET, COMPLIMENTED WITH DELIGHTFUL FOOD AND HOMEMADE PASTRY. THE FOLLOWING DAY, TRAIL OPTIONS, SOUTH, ALONG THE SHORE OF FALENSEE, WEST, OVER A PASS TO A KALEIDOSCOPE OF DISCOVERY INCLUDING A 4 – 5 HOUR TREK TO THE CLIFFSIDE BERGGASTHAUS AESCHER OR NORTH THROUGH A FOREST, RETURNING TO BRULISAU IN 3–4 HOURS.

BERGGASTHAUS STAUBERN

SAMTISERSEE

33

SAMTISERSEE

BERGGASTHAUS
BOLLENWEES
AND FALENSEE

BERGGASTHAUS AESCHER

34

THE EIGHT BEATITUDES OF JESUS

- "Blessed are the poor in spirit for theirs is the kingdom of heaven."

- "Blessed are they who mourn, for they shall be comforted."

- "Blessed are the meek for they shall inherit the earth."

- "Blessed are they who hunger and thirst for righteousness, for they shall be satisfied."

- "Blessed are the merciful, for they shall obtain mercy."

- "Blessed are the pure in heart, for they shall see God."

- "Blessed are the peacemakers, for they shall be called children of God."

- "Blessed are they who are persecuted for the sake of righteousness for theirs is the kingdom of heaven."

To overcome the negative subconscious mental influences, we must constantly be aware of God's love by plugging into his awaiting love with a heartfelt belief in the gospel and enjoy his peace with an active strong prayer life that includes thanksgiving and a peace that transcends all human understanding, guarding our thoughts, mind and heart in Christ Jesus. Philippians 4:6-7. My greatest treasure is God's love for me as that is where my heart will find peace and encouragement. Matthew 6:21, Romans 8:38-39. Express belief, for only with a strong overcomer belief and an apologetic stand will we be plugged into God's love. It is not what we feel but what we believe that is important. The book of Job substantiates this fact and that is what God has tried to tell us for the last 4000 years. Belief being our most important mindset. Include thanksgiving with all prayers. This displaces worry and gives one peace of mind. Ask people, "how do you believe? " Not "how do you feel? "

Material possessions or God's love? My greatest treasure is God's love for me, plugged into and following a heartfelt belief in the truth of the gospel. Matthew 6:21, "for where your treasure is," which is God's love, "there your heart will be also." 1st. Peter 1:18-19, "knowing that you were not redeemed with perishable things like silver or gold from your futile way of life inherited from your forefathers, but with **precious** blood as of a lamb unblemished and spotless, the blood of Christ." If your heart, source of thought is so guided with desire to please the one who loves you, then your thoughts, actions, habits, character and soul deposits will be rich and satisfying. You must stamp as an indelible reminder in your mind to be an overcomer to self, Satan and world influence, as God is the only one who unconditionally loves you. If God is the only one who unconditionally loves me, shouldn't my mind and thoughts be on him 24/7 the same as I experienced with my "first love?"

Apologetics are unique to humans. They represent God's plan of revealed logic. We were given eyes to see the evidence of **God's presence in control of all creation at this time**. We were given the gene of **conscience** to identify right and wrong. We were given the ability to know and record history as we were given **God's word** written over 1500 years by more than 40 individuals. Their minds, hands and fingers were guided by God and wrote with a common denominator of hope, the coming Redeemer **Jesus,** with the promise of eternal life, proof as a result of his **resurrection**. Our priority at this moment is to prepare now for conversation with the God of eternity, the cosmos, all creation, macro and micro as Jesus claimed, "Anyone who has seen me has seen the father." John 14:9. We realize this truth, yet shamefully avoid it. Prayer is our hinge, as it was with

36

Jesus. Remove the scales from your eyes, spiritual scales which are rusted in-situ from self as lord, Satan and world influence. These scales are removed when we believe the historical truth of the gospel through apologetics, God's gift. Think of the strong triple-braided cord, Ecclesiastes 4:12, "....a triple-braided cord is not easily broken," of the Trinity to assist you to overcome self, world and Satan, in the forward progress from seed to the metamorphosis of sanctification for conversion to a new birth. "For you must be born again," John 3:3, Ezekiel 36:25-27. The heartfelt presence of God's love and feeling his grace is our greatest motivator and treasure. 1st Thessalonians 5:16-18, "Rejoice always, pray without ceasing, and in everything give thanks, for this is the will of God in Christ Jesus for you." Philippians 4:6-7, "Don't worry about anything, instead pray about everything. Tell God what you need, with supplication and thank him for all he has done. Then you will experience God's peace, a peace that surpasses all human understanding which will guard your hearts, thoughts and minds in Christ Jesus."

The primary question for all people is: what happens following death? We all have a date with death, our time is very short - shorter by the hour. Our most important date is that moment of final judgment. How do I prepare for that appointment? I must prepare with the seed of the gospel before death. A true and valid belief is facilitated by a strong apologetic voice of logic and reason. A heartfelt implantation of God's love from trust in the gospel is the antidote for a destructive and corrupt soul that was poisoned and saturated by a long existing proclivity of total self-centeredness, Satan and world influence. God's indwelling love, the Holy Spirit, must daily embolden me to the overcoming of self, Satan and world influence.

The Lord is my shepherd. Not I am lord, but Jesus is Lord, and should be dictating my total thought, words and behavior if I am truly surrendered to him. Also if I truly believe, my thoughts will be influenced by the Beatitudes. God is always present, the Holy Spirit, by my identification with God's love, the cross of Christ. Visualize always being grafted into the Holy Spirit. Employ frequent communication through prayer, pray without ceasing. God's love for us is not dependent upon our belief in the gospel, however God's gift of conversion is from belief in the seed of the gospel. Living daily with the Holy Spirit, his love is the antidote to all fears and the only valid approach to effective psychotherapy. My dominant daily thought should be God's love for me. How many useless thoughts do I experience daily? Most surveys document that the majority of thoughts daily are negative, unproductive, filled with worry. With analysis of the 23rd Psalm, "he restores my soul." How is this accomplished? The re-education of my soul with surrender to Jesus as Lord and the Beatitudes as the foundation for thought and word "will lead me in the paths of righteousness, for his name's sake." God's love is always present, the Holy Spirit, if you have a heartfelt belief in Jesus. Thus you will have the confidence of eternal life and the expectation to "dwell in the house of the Lord forever," Psalm 23:6. With belief, we must plug into the awaiting socket of God's love. Revelation 3:20.   Carry your cross daily, which is death to self as lord and to identify with Jesus as Lord. Reject Satan and world influence and be an overcomer. Romans 6:4-7. Depend on the tri-fold cord of the Trinity to help you in all thoughts, God, the Holy Spirit, Jesus. Overcome your thoughts of self, Satan and world influence as a pattern of behavior. I desire the peace of God that transcends all

38

human understanding to guard my heart, mind and thoughts in Christ Jesus. Don't be anxious about anything, pray with supplication, be thankful. The end result is his promise of a peace that transcends all human understanding.

Can I speak about the reality of God, belief strengthened through a personal love relationship with Christ? Am I plugged into the ever-present reality of his stand-by love socket of Revelation 3:20? When you plug into the socket of belief in the gospel, the love of God is offered, that is, the birthing of the Holy Spirit into my heart. A love so precious and meaningful that I should experience the same degree of love as that described of the presence of a new life within my soul, identical to the joy of an expectant mother recognizing the first fetal movements. This equates to God's love for you. Revelation 3:20. I have had the privilege to assist for over a period of 30 years with the miracle and joy of delivering thousands of newborns to the breast of a loving mother. Each birth, an unbelievably precious experience. The same is true with the Holy Spirit birthing into a new believers soul for the indwelling fulfillment of spiritual rebirth. Indeed, both equally precious to the gracious recipients. Both result with obligations, responsibilities and a loving nurturing relationship. It is best to visualize a new birth in your soul rather than the receiving of a mature judgmental spirit to indwell you. Prayer is the connecting hinge in this relationship. Is the Holy Spirit always in my boat and heart or just a theoretic concept? Live constantly with the awareness of the presence of the Holy Spirit, a relationship of growth and maturation. To remain filled and victorious requires diligence and to keep all our mental chambers free of debris, not to impede his influence.

Love is our greatest personal emotional need with no exception. It is universal; every society, from those in the depths of the darkest jungles to the skyscrapers of Manhattan and Singapore. Everyone longs for someone to love them. I need to feel a stronger one-on-one with Christ. I must fix firmly with determined purpose, Jesus is Lord in my heart, and experience his omnipresent Holy Spirit and love. Believe and act as one with a personal Christ relationship. Fulfilled with **grace**. "**G**od's **R**iches **A**t **C**hrist's **E**xpense." You have nothing to lose. Live with an exclamation mark and not a question mark of insecurity. Revelation 3:20, Jesus stands at my door and knocks. Do I have deaf ears? I would be a fool not to respond. Love is there, I just need to connect with belief. Am I aware of God's love for me? Nothing is more rewarding than to know that someone loves you unconditionally. When I open the door of my heart with belief, I am grafted and "…. sealed in Him with the Holy Spirit of promise, who is given as a pledge of our inheritance, with a view to the redemption of God's own possession, to the praise of His glory." Ephesians 1:13-14. My mind must nurture and rest throughout the day that God formed me, knows me and loves me unconditionally. Psalm 139. I may be a pygmy or a Wall Street baron. Both equal in God's eyes. Multiple proofs are in the Bible and is a major theme. Unless we believe in Jesus we are unaware of his love. His love is there but no personal awareness unless belief and the acceptance of the Holy Spirit into our heart.

Rest your beliefs on God's gift of the epiphany of apologetics, sanctify Christ as Lord in your heart. Always be ready to give the reason for the hope that is in you. Christ has died. Christ has risen. Christ will come again. Two of these three prophesied events have been fulfilled. The third could occur any day. Enjoy the reassurance of God's love. Feel God's love for you in your heart dependent upon the truth of **general** and **specific apologetic revelation**. Believe in Jesus as Lord. All of **creation** is the evidence of God's presence at this moment. **Conscience**, an expression from our DNA, is the evidence of our need to relate to the moral parameters set by God. In the gospel, **Jesus** claimed to be equal with God, "he who has seen me has seen the Father." **Resurrection** proof, Simon of Cyrene, the Roman bystander, was compelled to carry the cross of Jesus. His sons Alexander and Rufus became believers and were active in the church from the witness and testimony of their father to the resurrection. This is referred to in Mark 15:21 and gives us additional confidence in the truth of the resurrection. The **Bible**, written over a period of 1500 years by 40 different authors, was designed to give us hope through a Redeemer and the anticipation of eternal life. John 3:16-17, Romans 8:37-39. God's love and presence is secure. God designed us to understand each area of apologetics and to enjoy hope, love, joy and peace as a result of personal application through faith. Romans 15:13. Sanctify Christ as Lord in your heart. You must first have a heartfelt belief of the truth of apologetics, that is; the cosmic ruling God and Jesus our redeemer as equal and plug belief into the always present awaiting socket of God's love for you. Revelation 3:20. We must replace self, Satan and world influence as false idols of worship with the only valid source of love, Jesus is Lord. His love is represented by his suffering and death on the cross for you and me.

Human love is fragile and fickle. Even those whose love for you is determined by commitment will be challenged by temporal feelings from the sensory reflex systems of the lower brainstem. With God,

41

commitment is solid following our belief in the gospel and responding to Revelation 3:20. Very simple, do you believe apologetics or ignore them? I want them to dominate my thoughts. I want Christian apologetic roots to bore deep into my core, impossible to extract. There is no other source of hope for eternal life, joy and peace other than belief in Christ, his omnipresence and love. If we ignore a rebirth prior to our physical death, our final judgment puts us into the second death, the lake of fire, eternal damnation. Thus, we must now, immediately, address our current corrupt soul and belief of self as God, before physical death. Following our belief in a Jesus as Lord conversion, from the gift of his grace, we will have faith, not fear, and must be diligent in our eternal fellowship with prayer. "No fears or anxiety, but prayer with supplication, thankfulness, and the peace of God that transcends all human understanding will guard our hearts, minds and thoughts in Christ Jesus." Philippians 4:6-7.

Be in the habit stating aloud from a heart belief, "Jesus is Lord." This statement has historically been expressed as an important creed to Christians for 2000 years. In 1498 Portuguese explorer Vasco da Gama sailed to Kerala, India to establish the first European Indian trade route for spices of pepper, cardamom and cinnamon. Kerala is a state on the southwestern tip of India with 600 km of Arabian Sea shoreline. It is a rich producer of spice agriculture. When Vasco da Gama arrived in Kerala he was surprised to find a thriving culture of Syrian Christians who claimed Christian heritage from 52 A.D. The current population of Kerala is 34 million people with 55% Hindu, 27% Muslim, and 18% Christian. It has long been the custom of the Syrian Christians of Kerala to speak immediately upon a birth, the first words in the newborn's ear, "Jesus Christ is Lord." It is their belief that these first words whispered in the ear of the newborn will establish a strong neural pathway, and as repeated over time to the child to adulthood will reinforce their thought and behavioral priorities. This vocalization to their newborns is still in practice today, an important tradition in their culture. In many additional geographical areas of the Christian world today, "Jesus is Lord" is a phrase of greeting and farewell. "If you confess with your lips that Jesus is Lord you will be saved." Romans 10:9. "No one can say Jesus is Lord except by the Holy Spirit." 1st Corinthians 12:3. "Now Is the time for salvation." 2nd Corinthians 6:2. It is too late after physical death. Only Christ offers hope following death. Romans 15:13. Do I reflect the presence of the Holy Spirit in my daily behavior? Do I really trust Jesus? How does my life reflect this? Do I demonstrate the fruit of the Spirit daily? Love, Joy, Peace, Longsuffering, Gentleness, Goodness, Faith, Gentleness, Temperance (self control). What did I do today that only a Christian would do?

If I currently do not have an enjoyable, intimate relationship with Jesus, how can I expect to enjoy heaven? We all need to believe something. If I'm wrong, it does not make any difference. If I'm right, then it makes a tremendous difference, an eternal difference. Live with joy in your heart. I would rather trust Jesus than any other person in the history of the world. We all have to trust someone or something. No one knows what happens at death. Who else apart from Christ and his resurrection, the evidence for this being overwhelmingly powerful, can give us any solid hope for the future? There is no one. One day we all must die and then what? Sadly, why miss out on a real love relationship now? When God made humans, he put eternity in our hearts as a foundational axiom and gave us the spiritual capacity to communicate with him through our redemption, identifying with the death of Jesus on the cross. Jesus came down the ladder to us. We did not have to climb the ladder carrying "works of achievement and righteousness" to him. Ephesians 2:8-10, "For by grace you have been saved through faith; and not of yourselves, it is a gift of God; not as a result of works, so that no one may boast." Romans 5:1-2, "Therefore, since we have been declared righteous by faith, we have peace with God through our Lord Jesus Christ." Jesus went to the cross for us even though each of us is still infested with the ugly disgusting worm of torment and sin, as an apple may appear beautiful on the outside but contains an unwanted intruder. We can be an overcomer by faith. My faith is dependent upon the historical Jesus and his claim to be equal with God. If he knew his statements to be a lie, he would not have died for a lie. He had many opportunities to change his path that led to the cross.

Is God real in your life? What quality of welcome do you want at the judgment seat? No action on our part is mandated, I either feel God's love or not. It all rests on God's gift of belief based on the truth, logic and reason of apologetics. "For God so loved the world that he gave his only Son, that whosoever believes in him shall not perish but have eternal life." John 3:16. If Christ is valid, then I must allow the seed of belief to impact my soul for metamorphosis, sanctification, with the fruit of belief expressed through the Holy Spirit as an anticipated verification. The book of James. Galatians 5:22, "love, joy, peace, patience, kindness, goodness, faithfulness, gentleness and self control." This is the fruit ripened and expressed as a result of beautiful progressive sanctification. In the absence of the Holy Spirit our fruit is self-serving and hypocritical. Our faith is measured by the action of the Holy Spirit to produce the fruit of the Spirit through us.

God designed the communion service to illustrate his purpose for coming to earth and leaving, taking mankind's sin to the cross for those who would believe and trust in him then and in the future. He knew he was leaving and with this illustration wanted the apostles to always remember his existence and the purpose of the cross. His words "take in remembrance of me" were to reinforce his purpose, coming to earth. Communion is totally a personal matter, either you believe or not. God's love for mankind is represented by his bloodied body on the cross, which metaphorically is represented by the wine and the unleavened or "sinless" bread. Only if Jesus is Lord in your heart, if we really believe, then we can be assured of his unconditional love and mercy for us. You can explain, but cannot force a person to believe. We will act accordingly and will want to please God beginning with our thinking. The Beatitudes are to establish our new thought paradigm of words, actions, habits, and soul regeneration. My thoughts and behavior need to reflect the Beatitudes. Establish a habit to incorporate each Beatitude to daily behavior and deed.

Christ has died, Christ has risen, and Christ will come again. Two out of the three have been completed. When we take the bread and wine, we must feel in our heart identification with the death of our sins on the cross, our love relationship and the total picture of apologetics to reinforce belief. Nothing can separate us from God's love. 2nd. Corinthians 5:14-21. Romans 8:38-39. Jesus as God proved his love for us with his sacrifice, taking our sins on him, nailed and bloodied to the cross. The tightly woven temple curtain, representing our sin barrier to God, was torn open as a result of Christ's death on the cross. No one is without sin and needs redemption, repentance and conversion, a new birth, based on belief. Romans 3:9-18.

The bread representing his body and the wine representing his blood is to remind us of his sacrificial love for us on the cross. This visual should be always present as we face each day. Jesus should be in constant thought as he is truly the only one who loves us unconditionally, but to be aware, we must believe in our hearts that Jesus is our Lord. We must believe, even in the absence of feeling his presence. Think of the constant questioning from Job and his ultimate fulfilled joy, hope and gift of family and possessions.

Why did Christ choose bread and wine to remember him? The answer, Christ desired that we remember him at least at every meal we eat. A personal recall multiple times a day. Wine was common at every meal. Jesus as God proved his love for us as a sacrifice taking our sins on him bloodied and nailed to the cross. No one is without sin. Everyone needs a savior as our conscience proves our corruption. God did not want us to be robots responding to a preprogrammed element but desired a heartfelt trust and belief from our mind, heart and spirit, that he be Lord instead of self.

Belief is a gift from God. Through logic and reason, apologetics provide the avenue to experience a heartfelt belief in the gospel and an on-going love relationship with Jesus through the Holy Spirit. Don't be on the outside of a window looking at Jesus, knowing about him, with no personal contact. We must be open to his lordship and constantly feel his breath on us. Communion as a reminder of the cross which represents the availability of God's love for a believer. An overcomer is one who rejects self, Satan and world influence. His source of motivation and thought dependent solely upon belief in the gospel. With this heartfelt belief dominating our thoughts, we are plugged into the always awaiting socket of God's love. The cross represents his love. This is the answer for all negative thoughts, guilt, despair and hopelessness. To acknowledge God's love, we will desire to achieve God's expectations of us. The Beatitudes represent God's desire for the foundation of our thoughts.

For hopelessness, sanctify Christ Jesus as Lord in your heart and always be ready to give the reason for the hope that is in you. Hope is dependent upon strong apologetics resulting in belief, a gift from God. I must have apologetics on my tongue. The maker of the stars loved us so much that he would subject himself to torture and death desiring that we be with him for eternity. If you truly experience the omnipresence of God's love, the Holy Spirit, it is impossible to experience fear. How can my confident hope, Jesus is Lord, be expressed as a dominant trait of my personality? The answer, Psalm 16, a source of abundant hope, joy and confidence. How can I reflect apologetic general and specific revelation to direct my thoughts? Most people are held captive to self doubt, Satan and world standards of thought and not on the truths of Christian apologetics. We must be overcomers and our thoughts filtered and determined as a result of Jesus as Lord. There is only one source of unfaltering permanent love for us. Psalm 16:5-11 is a prayer of confidence. "Lord, you are all I have, no one else, you give me all I need, your love. My future is in your hands, I am always aware of the Lord's presence, he is near and nothing can shake me. I am thankful and glad and I feel completely secure because you protect me from the power of death, and the one you love, you will not abandon to the world of the dead. You will always show me the path that leads to life and your presence fills me with joy and brings me pleasure forever." A set sail determines our direction and our final destination, therefore set your soul as the sail of a ship steering with diligence for the desired ultimate eternal safe harbor, heavens glory.

One ship drives east
And another drives west
With the selfsame winds that blow.
Tis the set of the sails
And not the gales
Which tells us the way to go.
Like the winds of the sea
Are the ways of fate,
As we voyage along through life:
Tis the set of a soul
That decides it's goal,
And not the calm or the strife.

—Ella Wheeler Wilcox

The only way to not be anxious is to know God's love and the only way to know his love is by plugging into the awaiting socket of God's love with the strong heartfelt belief of Jesus as Lord, a gift from God through apologetics. This is a seed to be planted in my soul for metamorphosis and sanctification. This must take place before physical death. With physical death, the soul either goes to heaven or hell. There is no second chance. Think of Lazarus and the rich man. Luke 16:19-31. Therefore,"Do not be anxious about anything, but in everything pray with confidence and with supplication, include thanksgiving and the confidence of God's peace that transcends all human understanding will guard your heart, thoughts, and mind in Christ Jesus." Philippians 4:6-7.

Do I really know his love, the cross, the Holy Spirit? No other love exists so solid and permanent and therefore must be a top priority, every moment to enjoy. No human will ever love you as does Jesus, recognized following a heartfelt belief, the gift of God, an epiphany through apologetics. Jesus should be seen as the greatest reality in my life. I have been given grace in my relationship with Jesus and I should be motivated to share my experience. I was hellbound, tied to a corpse of sin leaning over the abyss and rescued through this gift of the epiphany of apologetics.

That is, Jesus was not just a historical figure meandering in sandals for 3 years in central Israel preaching good thoughts. He is present today, in control of the universe and in the soul of every true believer. He is accomplishing his goal of John 3:15-18, "that whoever believes may in Him have eternal life. For god so loved the world, that He sent His only begotten son, that whoever believes in Him should not perish but have eternal life. "For God did not send the son into the world to judge the world, but that the world should be saved through Him. He who believes in Him is not judged; he who does not believe has been judged already, because he has not believed in the name of the only begotten Son of God." From Jesus's own words, John 14:16-17, "And I will ask the Father, and He will give you another Helper, that He may be with you forever; that is the Spirit of truth, whom the world cannot receive, because it does not behold Him or know Him, but you know Him because He abides with you, and will be **in** you."

Peter, who should have faded to the shadows of obscurity from his denial of Jesus three times, instead by God's grace, which should be an encouragement to us, filled by the Holy Spirit recorded testimony in 1st. Peter 1:3-5, for 30 years filling his mind, writing, "Blessed be the God and Father of our Lord Jesus Christ, who according to His great mercy has caused us to be born again to a living hope through the resurrection of Jesus Christ from the dead, to obtain an inheritance which is imperishable and undefiled and will not fade away, reserved in heaven for you, who are protected by the power of God through faith for a salvation ready to be revealed in the last time."

The blood vessels on your head.

The Sun travels around the galaxy once every 200 million years - a journey of 100,000 light years.

A single human sperm cell contains around 37.5 MB of information.

"GOD HAD FUN WITH INTELLIGENT DESIGN"

"JOB'S TORMENTORS"...
SATAN

"REPLACEMENT THERAPY"
ORPHEUS AND THE SIRENS

"DILIGENCE"

KERALA, INDIA,
"JESUS CHRIST IS LORD"

This miracle of the process of spiritual metamorphosis, is a rebirth, shared with the miracle of your physical birth. I was the result of a one in four hundred trillion chance to be born. Included in this calculation are not only the various DNA possibilities of 1/ 200,000,000 sperm to impregnate one egg; but also the remote possibility of your mother and father meeting. You are important to God in both physical and spiritual birth. Are you ready for a miracle of spiritual rebirth? If God can do it for John Newton, a hard headed, rough and tough overly imbibing sea captain of the Atlantic slave trade from 1748 to 1754, when God pulled him away to study theology. He can do it for you and me. In 1773 Newton wrote *"Amazing Grace"* to illustrate a sermon and this beautiful song has provided solace for 250 years.

> *"Amazing grace, how sweet the sound*
> *That saved a wretch like me*
> *I once was lost, but now am found*
> *T'was blind but now I see....."*

Again, are you ready for a miracle? What's holding you back? God is waiting. Two more that reward and bring joy to the heart:

> *"Out Redeemer Lives"*

> *"Put Your Hand In The Hand Of The Man From Galilee"*

Christian maturation;

1. "Take all thoughts captive to the obedience of Christ." 2nd Corinthians 10:5

2. Filter all my thoughts, prior to expression with Philippians 4:8.

3. Practice thought replacement therapy with edifying thoughts pleasing to God and of eternal value.

4. Develop edifying visual images from the Word.

5. Establish scripture memory from strong biblical neural pathways with thought construction to be transmitted as words, actions, habits, character, a new soul, with eyes fixed upon a new secured eternal destiny. Psalm 119:11, "Thy word have I hid in mine heart, that I might not sin against Thee."

Do I have abundant hope in the face of death? Why settle for less. I should have joy which is "the outward expression of inner spiritual confidence" and show it, as I know my final destination. With sanctification, metamorphosis of the seed of God's love, righteousness should be evident. My backup is 1st John 1:9 when I fall. At all times carry Jesus Christ, faith as my shield of armor held in proper upright defensive position, Ephesians 6:16. Despair is the result of poisoned, sin piercing arrows constantly accessing the soul. Never lay down the shield of faith as if habitually unprotected, despair breeds the plague of spiritual discouragement, defeat, hypocrisy and failure, Satan's joy. Components of Psalm 23 should be very real to me daily. "Though I pass through the valley of the shadow of death I will fear no evil as Thou art with me." No one else can offer me complete forgiveness. No one else can be with me day and night throughout my life including all the valleys of the shadow of death. No one else can give me a new heart and a new life. Ezekiel 36:24-27. There is, and was, no one like Jesus.

Always be aware of his presence, the Holy Spirit. Visualize the Holy Spirit as the loyal, fully equipped Sherpa porter and mountain guide always at your side. He is completely dedicated to carrying your heaviest burdens for a successful journey, staying awake during the night to guard and protect you. He gathers wood to provide warmth, protection and safety while you sleep. I have total confidence and assurance that he will be there with the first morning light. He advises when to rope up in anticipation when passing over dangerous life threatening terrain. He allows us to make the choices, but we know his advice is best, the perfect path to take to avoid danger and he will never abandon us. Truly my God-given Paraclete. Psalm 31. I am dedicated never to grieve him. Romans 8:38-39, "for I am convinced that neither death nor life, neither angels nor demons, neither the present nor the future, nor any powers, neither height nor depth, nor anything else in all creation, will be able to separate us from the love of God that is in Christ Jesus our Lord." Identify with the Book of Job.

Look daily at all creation as it glorifies God, every bird, whales breaching in play in Ma'alaea Bay, trees, flowers, distant views of expectation across an ever changing deep blue sea. Whatever is pleasing to our eye, thank the creator. When in doubt, or tempted, think apologetics, God created all, Jesus is Lord. God removed the blinders of disbelief. Speak up. Believe he is with you.

If we feed our souls regularly on God's word, several times each day, we should become robust spiritually, stronger to overcome hypocrisy bubbling up from our subconscious. Nothing is more important than hearing and obeying the Word of God. Psalm 119:11, "Thy word have I hid in mine heart, that I might not sin against thee." Become robust in spirit. Do I feed my soul with world, flesh, devil, temporal or eternal values? Garbage in, garbage out. "Lord help me to feed exclusively on eternal truth, not temporal." I need to feed on God's word three times daily to have a robust spirit to defeat my ubiquitous worm of hypocrisy. The minimal dose for a therapeutic spiritual blood level. Philippians 4:4-9, Galatians 5:22. Encourage people God is with them as they experience belief. Do they admit to the truth of apologetics and believe in the undeniable historic validity of Jesus and the total gospel? This belief is the basis of conversion, regeneration, to be born-again, death to self, the seed of belief to be implanted into our soul. Metamorphosis of the spirit and soul is followed by faith. Belief is first, followed by faith and trust. Sanctification is a result of metamorphosis from the seed of belief of Jesus as Lord. I may not feel God's presence but I should be confident he is there, as he was with Job. His love and his presence, the Holy Spirit, is experienced by faith.

My ethos exudes expression from the riches or corruption of the soul. A corrupt soul, thus a corrupt ethos and spirit dominated by self, Satan or worldly infusion and influence. Galatians 5:19-21. What people **SEE** in you, in less than 60 seconds, your ethos, shouts so loud they do not hear your words. I desire to express an ethos of evidence of reconciliation with God. The presence of his grace. Strength and confidence. 2nd. Corinthians 5:18-21. Contemporaries desire to see an entry to criticize their own faults and weaknesses as seen in you, to feel superior. They want to see you with more faults than themselves. Be on guard as they will tempt and test you desiring to see and hear a response inconsistent with Christian thought. They will respect you if they do not see a mirror image of their own self-inflicted issues. Thus so important that in looking at you, they see a person with one eye on the presence of God, transparency and diligence to righteousness. The other eye on a valid concern and attention to their presence. They desire empathy not hypocrisy. We should be looking at people with compassion for their handicaps, medical, social or lost spiritual condition. We either live with fear, which is unhealthy, or faith, which promotes health. With sudden fear there is an increased production of cortisol associated with a fight or flight response. A chronic elevated base level of cortisol promotes unhealthy stress to all our organs. We are programmed to handle sudden episodes of stress in an emergency but not programmed physiologically to handle prolonged elevated base levels. We must treat with Philippians 4:6-7, prayer with thanksgiving and a peace that transcends all human understanding. This should be our immediate response to anxiety and stress. I must wear belief and God's love for me, the Holy Spirit, as a protective armor, a palpable and visible mantle. Ephesians 6:10-18. The presence of God's love is stronger than any fear. Fear unchecked will have psychological and physiological consequences negative to health. Wrap yourself daily with the cloak of the Holy Spirit.

God made our subconscious to store past events and thoughts that lie just below our consciousness, 50-80% of all storage. Below this in the deeper recesses, is the unconscious, representing 30-40% of stored information of our past events. This is the area of repressed memory that we cannot selectively pull up for recall without hypnosis, drug inducement or a spontaneous sudden trigger event or thought. Our conscious mental state is said to contain only 10% of current thought. The conscious mind gives the subconscious sector instructions of what to recall. The three sectors can be reprogrammed only as a result of a determined, diligent, strong program of thought, from top down, for a change at the core level, our unconscious. The only way to affect change in the subconscious and unconscious for subsequent recall is with the dominant presence and work of the Holy Spirit and our greater dependency on God's words to influence our thoughts. More time spent on rumination and memorizing from the Word to organize our thoughts. For best results our storage chambers should be as filled to maximum as is the average commercial self-storage unit. Maximum capacity, with excess junk thoughts removed to allow for the more valuable thought storage. This desire for righteous thoughts should motivate us for a constant dependence and fellowship with the Holy Spirit, as Jesus promised as our Paraclete. He knew well the mental difficulty we would experience in the absence of total commitment to his Lordship and our need for the Holy Spirit. During quiet times the subconscious fed by the unconscious will haunt you with insecurity and fear, as it bubbles to the surface and expressed to conscious thought. Imagination loves to breed and feed on fear. If God designed and made the cosmos, certainly he designed all life and planned that we as humans have the spiritual capacity with the ability for deprogramming unconscious and subconscious influence to our thoughts and behavior. How is this accomplished? As Sigmund Freud dictated, man's thought and behavior is the product of our unconscious and subconscious storage. Luke 6:45, "the good man brings good things out of the good stored up in his heart, and the evil man brings evil things out of the evil stored up in his heart. For out of the overflow of his heart, his mouth speaks."

Understanding the influence of the unconscious and subconscious mind is key to understanding the power of biblical meditation for success in replacement therapy as applied to these sectors. Both are empty at birth and are progressively filled as storage chambers for significant emotional thoughts and experiences throughout our lifetime. The unconscious stores primarily undesirable thoughts and experiences, repressed to voluntary recall. Our subconscious is 24 hours a day at work normally from conscious request, playing back subconscious thoughts to the conscious mind, influencing our thoughts and behavior. Our unconscious and subconscious can be reprogrammed only following **total** surrender of all our mental chambers to the lordship of Christ, with the presence of the Holy Spirit and our persistent diligence. An encouraging thought is to remember, with diligence, the snail made it to the Ark. Our diligence to biblical meditation with rumination is imperative, as a cow chewing its cud. We must repeat scripture over and over in our minds, understand what it is actually saying and let it sink deeply in our minds for subsequent recall. Memorizing scripture without ruminating is not successful meditation for successful mental implantation. Scripture can be memorized without ruminating, however ruminating is the key for establishing a strong memory bank for successful reprogramming of our unconscious and subconscious, from top down, thus to achieve new dominant neuro pathways. With this established as habit, ruminating on scripture, over time, we will recall pertinent scripture of a stronger neural pathway for the conscious replacement in lieu of undesirable thoughts awakened from the unconscious or fed from the subconscious.

If Jesus knew he was a lie, he would not have sacrificed to death for a lie. God went to the cross on purpose for me. Do I deserve it? No, no one does. John 3:16 represents God's love for man, desiring our heartfelt belief. Jesus, by claiming to be God, subjected himself to persecution. Jesus could have avoided the cross by denial of his claims of deity. If Jesus was just a man he would not have gone to the cross in shame and ridicule for a lie. We know that we need him. We are otherwise in denial. Jesus knew the importance of his crucifixion. How can we not respond appropriately?

Death is not the end. Death is only putting out the lamp at the rise of a new dawn. The "new dawn" can metaphorically be described as experiencing the effect of the first rays of sunrise while perched on a cold and damp frost-covered slippery boulder outside the 9,000 foot mountain top Swiss Faulhorn Berghaus at 5 A.M. in the moist, cold August morning air. At an exact moment the tallest most magnificent distant mountain peak awakens first, touched by the first rays of light from God's emerging dome of fire, then with a domino effect, other sleeping giants are set aglow in a pattern that certainly other life forms have witnessed for millions of years, candles set aglow. The embracing asymmetrical foundations of massive glacial ice are next to radiate a mysterious blue glow. As God awakens each alpine peak, the promise of a new day, reassurance and optimism to embrace the blessed observer.

When the turbulence of doubt and fear appear, our faith can be secured on the rock of Christ. Secure as firmly attached "hold-fast" roots of tall seaweed stalks stretching to the surface seeking sunlight from the rocky ocean floor. With strong counter-torque forces in the demanding currents, yet the "hold-fast" of faith remains firmly attached in the presence of storms raging above.

When we have doubts think of the validity of the cross and resurrection. If true, then the Holy Spirit is present as promised, his love, and our endowment of eternal life. We must have faith in something. We have to trust something or someone about the future, not ourselves as a final endpoint. In the absence of conversion, eternal damnation to the soul is guaranteed. Our physical atoms return to the physical world to be recycled. If Christ lives, then he lives in me by my total trust in Jesus as Lord, not myself as lord. This truth must replace my totally self-centered thoughts, if I desire to please God, the only one who unconditionally loves me. Vocalize with habit, "Jesus is Lord," as the Syrian Christians of Kerala have practiced this beautiful tradition for nearly 2000 years. When challenged with doubt, visualize immediately an apologetic cause with full confidence, the evidence of God's presence in creation, conscience, Jesus, the Gospel and God's word. Doubt leads to fear. We tend to imagine and visualize the worst scenario. In troubling times visualize God's love for you, Christ on the cross and his embrace. Romans 1:16, "For I am not ashamed of the gospel of Christ, for it is the power of God to salvation for everyone who believes, for the Jew first and also the Greek."

On what evidence does our belief rest? He would not have subjected himself to torture if his claims were a lie. Belief is the seed for conversion for our souls, metamorphosis, sanctification, a process of progressive holiness. Sprinkle with 1st. John 1:9 for recovery of confidence when we fall. Without belief, our soul is headed for the second death. From Psalm 30, "tears may flow in the night but joy comes in the morning." God's word is a wonderful protection from dreadful imagination, death and eternal torment. The goal and purpose was designed to promote confidence and hope through belief in a coming redeemer fulfilled in Jesus Christ. Romans 15:4, 12 -13.

Have belief based on apologetics and not feelings before I give a statement or response. Is my response the result of a sensory lower brainstem reflex or the result from the cerebral cortex incorporating wisdom? What should elevate my soul most? Answer, to think on the person who loves you unconditionally. The God who made the cosmos and all life, chose me, one out of 200 million sperm, to be conceived on or near July 4th, 1935, with one of the 450 eggs ovulated during my mother's reproductive lifetime. As mentioned, the chances of being born considering all the variables, starting with your mother meeting your father and DNA possibilities, has been estimated at 1 in 400 trillion. Psalm 139. Give others full attention, they are equally important in the eyes of God. Think of this for motivation to share what God has given you in grace. Withhold an expression of prejudice and see people as God sees you, with compassion and forgiveness. Who could love you more than someone nailed on a cross with you in mind, and I turned him down? Satan's pleasure is that you doubt this historic fact of total redemption simply through a heartfelt life changing belief and faith.

What has greater control over my actions, belief or feelings? The endpoint for feelings results in failure as many times proven. Galatians 5:19-21. Contrasted to the endpoint of Jesus is Lord, results in unlimited expectations and a valid hope of eternal life. God's love is omnipresent. Think of Job. God never promises to save us from suffering, he does promise to be with us in the midst of it. This is one purpose of the book of Job, the reassurance of God's omnipresence. The greatest test of a Christian's life is to live with the silence of God. Our thoughts, however must rest on apologetics. The evidence of His presence. When in doubt, think on apologetics, the endpoint, God's love and constant presence. Even when all is dark and silent, still we know that God is there, his word never broken, his steadfast love never fails. We know he is there because of general and specific apologetic revelation. That is; evidence of his presence and purpose in creation, conscience, the gospel and God's word. The greatest source of nourishment for health and care of the soul and body is to feed on the truth of God's love.

Two seasoned ministers, each with more than 40 years in the field, on different occasions stated in public their most profound thought to be; "Jesus loves me this I know, for the Bible tells me so." Good advice for frequent personal recall learned from childhood.

Do not grieve the Holy Spirit. This is a result of failing attention to the Holy Spirit, rejection of the Holy Spirit, basically unbelief. The cardinal unforgivable sin. How is my confidence in the presence of Jesus, Holy Spirit, challenged? By not feeling his presence. True of Job and the Psalms. Gain and strengthen reassurance with apologetics and thanking God for all apologetic proofs of his constant presence, with prayer to Jesus and promises in the Bible. It's all very simple and obvious. We were given free will with the proclivity for evil, a result of self as number one. God made us with a plan for spiritual eternal fellowship and provided a Redeemer for the corruption controlling our souls by a heartfelt belief in Jesus as Lord. Belief, a result of our free will and God's plan, is required to plug into the awaiting socket of his love. Revelation 3:20, and the story of the Prodigal Son. We are to enjoy a love relationship now and for eternity. Do I love Jesus as my Shepherd and King or do I vacillate from "feelings" and lack total commitment? Diligence must be enforced as our old nature yearns to regain dominance from temptations daily.

Not that I know scripture, but does scripture know me? Does scripture indwell me? "Thy word have I hid in my heart, that I might not sin against thee." Psalm 119:11. Scripture memory and recall is my strongest weapon combined with experiencing the presence of the Holy Spirit and staying protected in the armor of Ephesians 6:10-18, to successfully walk the path of "The Way."

The imaginations of our mind are what we become. Proverbs 23:7, "as a man thinketh in his heart, so is he." Philippians 4:8, "Finally, brothers and sisters, whatever is true, whatever is noble, whatever is right, whatever is pure, whatever is lovely, whatever is admirable – if anything is excellent or praiseworthy – think about such things." Again, to win the battle over self requires diligence to mind focus.

Valid belief requires evidence of submitting to the Lordship of Christ in my life. The Creator of the universe loves you, desiring that you submit to him as boss. We live as beggars with unfulfilled desires for someone to love us until we experience a total heartfelt belief in Jesus as Lord and fellowship with the Holy Spirit. When you know with confidence that someone loves you totally and unconditionally, we have the greatest source of motivation to please that person, to seek and accomplish their expectations for you. The God of hope, joy and peace loves you. Romans 15:13, Revelation 3:20, the story of the Prodigal Son. God put agape, unconditional love, in our hearts to be enjoyed. "Agape love" is the power that moves us to respond to someone's needs with no expectation in return. Therefore make use of this with God and people. Think of someone you have known that possessed this virtue and the impact their lives enjoyed. Is my "agape" gene dormant? A gift from God. Satan desires that it stays dormant, repressed. How often do I express unconditional love? Make it a habit, with transparency, a trademark of your personality. Beware of acting on feelings.

The lower brainstem sensory receptors reflect robotic reflexes. Do not live from the lower brainstem reflexes but from belief, through the cerebral cortex with logic, reason, influx. This is the manifestation of wisdom. Walk by belief, not by sight. Base your belief totally on apologetics. Avoid responding to feelings. Every thought should be captive to the obedience of Christ prior to speech or action. Belief should dictate my thoughts, fortified by God's love. Apologetics are the

64

entry gate to belief, approached with an open mind of logic and reason.

However long or short my life might be, nothing is more profound or important than knowing that God loves me. Must be at the apex of thought. The mainsail to stay on course. Romans 8:35-39. Even though his presence is not felt, I must rest assured from apologetic belief, his love, the cross, and his resurrection. Don't flounder with insecure and unstable "feelings" but by the foundational belief of God's love for you. Otherwise we tend to be slaves in bondage to our feelings. Humans are self-engrossed and reluctant to submit totally to the Lordship of Christ, Satan's delight. Based on your belief in the gospel, nothing negative can compete with the power of God's unconditional love. With apologetics, if you believe the evidence of the controlling presence of the God of creation and his genetic gift of conscience, we must believe the logic and truth of the gospel. Jesus claimed "he who has seen me has seen the Father." Look at the universe and see Jesus and the Creator of the cosmos as one entity. Should be in **constant** daily recall for thought and walk as I desire that this thought float and stay permanently on the surface as cream in freshly obtained farm milk and not homogenized.

WE need to walk by a belief in Jesus as Lord. Look in a mirror and see Jesus as Lord and God's love for you. Do not rely on love from a human, you will be disappointed. Moment by moment experience God's love, especially when under attack from self doubt, the devil, or criticism from the world. Human love is fickle, superficial, easily altered. Don't rest on the love from people. Walk by belief, not by feelings. I should be alerted and aware when I am a slave to feelings; a red alert, 911, code blue, tsunami warning of a high pitch siren. It's not feelings that are important but belief. John 3:16, "for God so loved the world that he gave his only begotten Son, that whosoever believes in him should not perish but have everlasting life."

Apply apologetics to this verse to make it real. I should do whatever is necessary to trust and believe to the inner parts of my body of God's authentic love for me. His sustained and unconditional agape love. Start with the totality of apologetics to prove the authenticity of Jesus as Lord. The overwhelming sense of the presence of God will elevate our spirits and a peace and security that transcends all human understanding. Always pray with thanksgiving.

Be transformed by the renewing of your mind. Romans 12:1-2. A strong belief must be evidenced by action to be valid. Jesus as Lord must rule our soul, every thought, word, behavior, habit, soul change and character. The most profound thought to renew your mind is to put God on the throne and remove self, therefore pass all thoughts through God's thought filter before speaking. That is, Philippians 4:8 "whatsoever is true, noble, right, pure, lovely, admirable, excellent and praiseworthy." My ethos will expose valid belief due to my expression of confidence of God's love for me. The ongoing thought of the reality of God's love for you will overcome and replace one's thoughts of failure. Only after we plug into God's love will we be motivated to reach the expectations that Christ has for us, as we must feel his "drive by" love to be motivated. As a desire to drive by the home of your first love, hoping to see or a chance encounter, a desire dependent upon rich, unselfish fellowship and thankfulness. We will not experience the love of God unless we have a heartfelt belief in the gospel. The stronger the belief to transform us, resulting from the epiphany of apologetics, the greater we feel his love. God's love is there for all people. We must admit that a person feels totally alive when he or she feels loved, the neurohormone influence. Express love and thankfulness throughout the day for God's presence. Belief in the gospel must overpower self-centeredness, Satan and worldly influence. We should not need to hear the Gospel over and over. We know in our hearts what we should believe, our pattern of thought, and what to avoid.

Satan and our old nature desire that we have deaf ears and hardened hearts. Does my ethos of joy express my confidence of God's love for me? My belief must be stronger than self doubt or failure in order to express this joy of spiritual confidence. We must experience a "Jesus as Lord" total surrender before the expectation of plugging into God's love to dominate our thoughts. Am I motivated to share the resurrection of Jesus, God's offer of grace and to speak apologetics as a habit? Romans 15:13, if we are truly filled with joy and peace, then it should be evident. Only through total trust, facilitated by the Holy Spirit. Memorize scriptures of faith and speak them. Do I carry the sword of the word of God with a dominant presence for active engagement, or held hidden in a sheath of concealment? Romans 1:16, "For I am not ashamed of the gospel for it is the power of God for salvation to everyone who believes, to the Jew first and also to the Greek."

We must be the one to plug into the socket of love and belief. Otherwise, it is only a distant fable and make-believe. All other religions of the world are man made and deviates from truth. All based on accomplishments, goals, and requirements, impossible to attain due to our human nature, thus held in bondage to guilt, fear and captives to an icon of unreality. The Cross of Christ is the only true spiritual path from God to man, not buildings, icons, formulas, mantras or any other historical fabrication from man. Throughout history, Satan has attempted to distort the truth of Jesus through control and tempting man's sin nature and self importance over submission to Jesus as Lord. This has occurred in all cultures and castes of society, with Satan successfully influencing through weakness, misconceptions, ignorance and prejudice of people groups in all periods of history.

Examples are seen repeatedly in Bible history, and later the crusades and Spanish inquisition. Satanic distortions of Christianity. Today, Satan has vast influence in all societies. This is why we must stay fixed on the Bible for truth and guidance, logic, reason, diligence and with clean minds, subject to the Holy Spirit.

Other examples of how Satan influences cultures. The more material possessions and excess comforts, the less we focus on eternal life and spiritual thoughts. We experience a spiritual disinclination qualified to our ease of life with attention to material satisfactions. Other cultures with little material advantage seek escape from life's daily difficulties, focused therefore on their cultic religious requirements, traditions, idols, ceremonies, superstitions and mantras to satisfy implanted thoughts of eternity. They are held in bondage with the belief of karma, that all that happens to them was meant to be, a result of personal and past generational sins. This ubiquitous thought process results in little motivation for hope of an upward trajectory to improve their global life status of recurrent famine, poor health and hygiene or the caste system of social standing, thus holding them in satanic bondage.

Missionaries I know who have worked in sub-equatorial African countries for many years verify this as to the basic impediment to reaching them with the gospel and motivate them for an improvement in living standards. The dominant belief, "that's the way it was meant to be." Even where inroads have been made and especially after a missionary is absent for a brief time, Christian dogmas are contaminated with karma influence. Adding to the problem has been the arrival of Islamic representatives paying off a local native "pastor" with either monetary bribes or intimidation that cannot be refused. In some cases buying the church and changing it to a mosque. The end result, that the karma influence prevails.

From personal experience in Nepal, the strength of the karma influence will appear when a family experiences tragedy or sickness, "a punishment from God." Those poor souls of the Hindu culture afflicted with leprosy, also known as Hansen's disease, are ostracized from the family so as not to be identified as related. As a result I met with little success even with the help of locals in attempting to supply newly developed diagnostic skin tests that would identify individuals previously exposed to the leprosy mycobacterium. The benefit, to be able to treat with antibiotics early, eradicating the organism prior to the eruption of gross disfigurement. Relatives and those of long close contact refused to even acknowledge knowing the afflicted. Christian inroads are difficult among these cultures. Christ was exposed to this in his day, yet encouraged his apostles and us not to give up but to preach his precepts, seeking a spiritual rebirth for all people. Matthew 28:19-20, "The Great Commission."

Faith is a living entity, it is born, it is viable and grows, or it dies. As with a plant, faith requires constant feeding. We must equally experience God's love in a real heart experience daily, not a vague concept, to feed our faith. This is dependent upon strong apologetic thinking. We can see God's love for us in the components of apologetics. Without God's love, our souls are spiritually dead. No rebirth, no metamorphosis, no faith. Hell will be the result. We have no one else to blame but ourselves. Do I really believe or is my soul dead? God's love is the antidote to fear, hopelessness and guilt and sustains our faith. Equate the power of spiritual light to the power of physical light on all life in the plant realm. Our faith also must have light, the presence of the word of God, Jesus. It is most important that we know God's love for us. He is spiritual light. The light from the sun provides electromagnetic energy for photosynthesis of otherwise dormant chlorophyll. God's light, Jesus provides the energy to our faith. We need daily inflow of God's light, Gods word, to the seed of belief in our soul for the metamorphosis of sanctification, conversion and sustenance for faith.

We must keep our minds and hearts filled with the fact of God's love for us, Psalm 139, otherwise we live in constant fear and expect the worst. Review truths in the Bible that give reassurance of God's constant personal love for us. Romans 8:37-39 and Ephesians 3:14-21 are excellent verses to memorize and enjoy with thoughtful rumination. Apologetics are also important to ponder on. Ask yourself, does God love you? The answer; John 3:16, "for God so loved the world

"A NEW DAY AWAKENS"

"SWISS
AND
CHAMONIX
TRAIL
VIEWS"

that he gave his only begotten Son, that whosoever believeth in him should not perish but experience everlasting life." Fear, superstition and anxiety dominate our thoughts unless we encourage active faith in God's love, our strongest antidote to fear and anxiety. God's love felt in our hearts is the result of a heartfelt belief plugged into the awaiting socket of God's love, Jesus standing at the door knocking, waiting for our response. Revelation 3:20. We may not feel God's presence but if the Bible is true, God's love and presence is in abundance. Belief must dominate over feelings. Our apologetics must be stronger than doubt. We must be an overcomer through a heart belief. It is difficult to accept God's love for us due to self-condemnation from past failures and long existing criticisms from self, Satan and the world. This is the reason that encouragement is so important for young and old. How can I give the most encouragement? Be a listener. The fastest, most pragmatic way to encourage, is by expressing respect, interest, love and to be a listener. Remind myself to avoid negatives and always look for ways to express honest encouragement. God's love in our hearts and Biblical reference is our best source of encouragement which quantitatively is dependent upon our belief. As mentioned earlier, Romans 15:13 provides a foundation of encouragement to rest upon.

Indeed, Paul left a legacy of encouragement everywhere he traveled. His ubiquitous greeting of grace and peace gives a clue to his daily interplay with people. Throughout his letters encouragement exudes. I had a dear pastor friend that passed away at the age of 64 of cancer. His funeral was attended by over 1,000 people and had to be held outside in a garden setting. He preached up to a few days before he passed on, never a complaint even though riddled with disease, and is never to be forgotten by those who knew him. His repetitious words to me at every meeting, "Ralph, I want to be just like you, you are my hero and best friend." I knew for sure that I would hear these words with every encounter. Now I don't know how many people he greeted this way but it didn't matter as I so much enjoyed each predictable friendly encouraging encounter. What a legacy he left as I think of him often, with a smile, his rich and authentic friendship. Jesus in John 15:12, "This is my commandment, that you love one another, just as I have loved you." Our goal should be to honor people and give praise. An easy start is to make a habit of telling people "grace and peace be with you," and mean it.

Biblical answers to specific torments that will yield encouragement:

Resentment.....I can't forgive."I can do all things through Christ who strengthens me." Philippians 4:13.

Fear....."God has not given us the spirit of fear, but of power and of love and of a sound mind." 2nd. Timothy 1:7.

Anxiety....."Cast all your anxiety on (Christ) because he cares for you." 1st. Peter 5:7. "Do not be anxious about anything." Philippians 4:6.

Discouragement...."This I call to mind and therefore I have hope. Because of the Lord's great love we are not consumed, for his compassions never fail. They are new every morning, great is your faithfulness." Lamentations 3:21-33. "Let us not become weary of doing good, for at the proper time we will reap a harvest if we do not give up." Galatians 6:9.

Isolation......"I (the Lord) will never leave nor forsake you." Hebrews 13:5.

Guilt....."There is now no condemnation for those who are in Christ Jesus." Romans 8:1.

Failure....."In all these things we are more than conquerors through him who loved us." Romans 8:37.

Stress....."In the world you will have tribulation; but be of good cheer, I have overcome the world." John 16:33.

Weary...."The Lord is the strength of my life." Psalm 21:7.

Opposition....."The one who is in you is greater than the one who is in the world." 1st. John 4:4.

Confusion....."God generously gives wisdom to those who ask him for it." James 1:5.

Lack of faith....."My God shall supply all your need according to His riches in glory by Christ Jesus." Philippians 4:19.

A strong belief must be experienced by action to be valid. Jesus as Lord must rule our soul, thus his input expressed with every thought, word, behavior, habit, soul and character exchange. The most profound thought to renew your mind is to put God on the throne and remove self, therefore pass all thoughts through God's thought filter before speaking. That is, Philippians 4:8, whatsoever is true, noble, right, pure, lovely, admirable, excellent and praiseworthy. Allow only thoughts with these virtues to pass through your thought filter prior to expression. Why do you not consistently practice what you preach? "Thank you my observant friend. I see that as you point one finger at me, three fingers are pointing in your direction." I am the first to admit defects in my cerebral filter and the need to remove debris from passing through. Each of these virtues will be analyzed in greater detail with a goal of more consistent responses to reflect these virtues over our immediate lower brainstem reflex responses.

In reference to whatsoever is:

"TRUE" is covered in Ephesians 4:25, to always speak the truth, no lying. John 17:17, Thy Word is truth, Ephesians 4:21, the truth is in Christ. In summary truth is found in the Word of God.

"NOBLE" is referenced in 2nd. Corinthians 8:21, be honorable toward God and man, respectful. Not trashy, mundane or common. Derived from a word meaning worship, thus whatever is worthy of adoration and respected. Held in high regard.

"JUST", righteous in act and word, Deuteronomy 16:19, to show no perversion of justice with bribes, honesty and justice to all men. Titus 1:8, self control. To think on what is absolutely consistent with the holiness of God.

"PURE", 1st. Timothy 5:22 and James 3:17, speech and behavior reflecting impeccable ethics. Morally pure, clean, undefiled. Not to think on trash. "Without holiness you will not see God", Hebrews 12:14.

"LOVELY", 1st. Corinthians 13:4-7, edifying love, the desire to uplift others, not focused on self edification, patient, kind, no jealousy, nor pride, not demanding your own way, not irritable, no grudges, love does not give up, never loses faith, always helpful, endures in every circumstance.

"GOOD REPORT", Admirable, commendable, kindly spoken, Derivation from Greek, "fair sounding", the safety of an ocean depth determination, evolving over time to an outward expression of "that which is lovely." Auspicious and acceptable.

"VIRTUE", 2nd. Peter 1:5, virtue is the energy to advance from faith to knowledge, reflecting a fruitful growth in faith. The reward is in the journey of a faith directed life, God enjoys our company. That which is excellent, beautiful and lofty.

"WORTHY OF PRAISE", references a behavior or action that deserves acclaim or celebration. It is praiseworthy to treat everyone with kindness, honorably, and admirably. If we desire a God pleasing speech and behavior, the above will be our priority to establish as a habit when confronted with a stimulus requiring a response.

These virtues recorded by Paul in Philippians 4:8 are those that God desires to pass through our thought filter to form thoughts and deeds.

William Glasser M.D., a secular psychiatrist, in his book, "Stations of The Mind "reinforces the idea that we are regressing to minds of lower animal forms. He calls it S-R, stimulus-response behavior. A response, "how does it make us feel and will it work?" This thinking has become more and more prevalent in our society, a "feel good "desire as the end point. Self first. The lack of Godly goals in determining our thoughts and behavior has led to a society with record numbers of psychiatric and social issues. In essence, this is a life dominated by the lower brainstem over the cerebral cortex.

Godly thoughts constantly ruminating in our minds are lacking as Paul impresses upon us to pursue. The world influence is winning, however if we desire the peace that transcends all human understanding, spiritual stability and fewer visits to the psychiatrist, discipline to Paul's instructions is imperative and the answer to society's problems.

We will not experience the love of God unless we have a heartfelt belief in the gospel. The stronger the belief to transform us, the greater we feel his love. God's love is there for all people. They just need to truly believe in Christ to be aware of it. Belief in the gospel must overpower self-centeredness, Satan and worldly influence. Must be a Jesus as Lord **total** surrender, before we can plug into God's love that will dominate our thoughts. No partial surrender. It is important that we express joy and praise to Jesus with the habit of thankfulness. Romans 15:13, "May the God of hope fill you with all joy and peace, in trusting him that you will abound in hope through the power of the Holy Spirit." To completely replace doubt, we must saturate completely our hearts with belief first, to be confident in God's love. Never pull the plug on belief, otherwise we can lose a conscious awareness of his love. God's love is the nourishment our souls require in the process of sanctification for a spiritual rebirth. Without experiencing God's love our souls will remain spiritually dead. No rebirth, no metamorphosis. Hell will be the result. We have no one else to blame but ourselves. Do I really believe or is my soul dead from long-standing self-imposed corruption and dominance of self-will? We must keep our minds and hearts filled with the fact of God's love for us, otherwise we live in constant fear, insecurity, and expect the worst. Review truths in the Bible that reassure us of God's constant personal love for us. Romans 8:37-39, Ephesians 3:14-21. Apologetics are so important for reassurance. Fear, superstition and anxiety dominate our thoughts unless we encourage an active faith in God's love, the greatest antidote to fear and anxiety. God's love felt in our hearts is the result of a heartfelt belief, plugged into the awaiting socket of God's love. Jesus standing at the door knocking, waiting for our response. Revelation 3:20. He does not break down the door, only that **WE** open the door with belief and trust to the awaiting Lord, the Holy Spirit. We may not feel God's presence but if the Bible is true, God's love and presence is in abundance. Belief must dominate over our feelings. Our apologetics must be stronger than doubt.

We can feel God's love if we reinforce our minds on the apologetics that bind the presence of God to the evidence and presence of Christ. General revelation is linked to specific revelation with the fact that Jesus repeatedly claimed to be equal with God. Paul's belief, motivation and passion was fueled by grace. This explains why Paul had no apparent residual guilt from his earlier persecution of Christians. He was confident of his forgiveness as a result of his personal contact with Christ. An experience that he repeated over and over. I suspect that even to close friends this story was told repetitiously, as a current love relationship is told and explained repeatedly to friends. Luke records Paul's conversion on the Damascus road in Acts 9. Paul also repeated in Acts 22 and again in Acts 26. This experience was responsible for the 180° change in his belief. As a result of this encounter and conversion he was subjected to a life of constant persecution and ridicule, however remaining loyal for 30 years with faith and proclaiming Christ during his 13,000 miles on sea journeys, Roman and dusty rural roads to his eventual death by martyrdom, A.D. 64-66. He left us with a wealth of history and spiritual encouragement with wonderful insight to the transparency and the inner workings of his mind with the Holy Spirit at work within his heart. How did Paul sustain hope and encouragement for those 30 years of life threatening trials and tribulations listed in 2nd. Corinthians 11:24-27? In 2nd. Timothy 4:7-8, knowing that he soon faced death "I have fought the good fight, I have finished the course, I have kept the faith; in the future there is laid up for me the crown of righteousness, which the Lord, the righteous Judge, will award to me on that day; and not only to me, but also to **all** who have loved His appearing." We are to experience the same hope and confidence of Paul as was ascribed by Tertius from Paul in Romans 15:13, "Now may the God of hope **fill** you with **all** joy and peace in believing, that you may **abound** in hope by the power of the **Holy Spirit.**" This is truly a life motivating verse, a source of hope and encouragement. A verse that I personally find beneficial for encouragement with frequent recall. We can also believe apostolic history as it is written and testified to from multiple sources of irrefutable extra-Biblical historic documentation. This is in addition to history written by the apostles and associates, substantiated by multiple sources through generations of scholarly research. My love for God should be so strong as a desire to be with him, reflecting upon belief and thus the desire to overcome self, Satan and world influence. We can only believe Jesus is Lord initially through an epiphany from apologetics followed by the gift of belief from God. The claims of Jesus' sovereignty bind and testify to the observations of general and specific apologetic revelation. This should awaken us to frequent recall of his intimate presence with you at this moment, the creator and maintainer of the cosmos and the Paraclete to our souls. The shadow of our existence.

Hebrews 6:19, "this hope we have as an anchor of the soul, my hope both sure and steadfast and one which enters before the veil in his presence." Jesus is the intermediary between man and God. If we do not experience a love relationship with Jesus now, how will we be content in heaven? Be an overcomer and be transformed, to experience and live with a spiritual influence dominating all thoughts. Not possible if the lower brainstem dominates my behavior and thoughts. We will not experience God's love unless a total surrender to the Lordship of Christ. Truly we are spiritual beings in an earth suit. Don't miss out on God's unconditional love. I want to have a love relationship now. He first loved us. See the need of my soul to be renewed and start with emptying old residual paradigms. "Sanctify Jesus as Lord in your heart and be prepared to give a reason for the hope you have in you, yet with gentleness and reverence." 1st Peter 3:15. Nothing is more important than our relationship with God at this time. Make a habit of repeating multiple times daily whatever strengthens your faith in God's love for you. Our inclination is not to meditate with purpose or consistency on God's love for us. Instead we are guilty of fleeting thoughts that do not burn an imprint on our souls. Tragically true, be diligent. The new birth allows us to see Jesus for who he really is, sets us free from the world and Satan, to allow God's love to activate and nourish our souls. We see the superior value of Jesus over everything else and must recall with unwavering diligence to live as an overcomer. Christ bleeding and dying on the cross. Belief in the presence of the torn veil providing our access to God, a result of the sacrifice of Jesus on the cross for the totality of the forgiveness of our sins and to experience a heartfelt fellowship with the Holy Spirit. Our eyes have been opened and we comprehend the treasure of belief in Jesus over the influence of Satan and the world.

Following conversion, God sees me in Christ as I walk the path of metamorphosis and sanctification. I am not paralyzed with hopelessness, fear, anxiety, defeat, depression or self-deprecation. The truth of the historical validity of Jesus and the gospel make our heart receptive to Jesus knocking at the door for love and fellowship, the promised endowment of the Holy Spirit. I should be a clay pot with the treasure of the light-giving gospel. Purpose is that the light be seen. Matthew 28:19-20. Only as a result of our new birth and experiencing the heartfelt presence of God's grace do we have a desire to invest in the souls of men as this is otherwise inconsistent with our old nature to have an interest in another's spiritual state. If we are not aware of God's living grace in our hearts, there is no authentic rebirth and no active interest in seeking the restoration of our fellow man's soul. You are still suffering from a hellbound disease of self. I suggest that you fall on your knees and "get right" with the creator of the universe, Jesus. Asking him into your heart and emptying all chambers of distracting unproductive foul debris. He has been standing at the door of your heart, knocking, knocking, knocking, with no serious response. Again, wake up before it is too late. He is waiting as a fisherman waits with hopeful expectancy for a reward that blesses him personally. Ephesians 1:3-10, "and it gave him great pleasure," Isaiah 53:10, "the pleasure of the Lord." We are formed extremely complex with 100 trillion neuron connections just in the brain, planned and designed by God. Our spirits and souls were also designed beyond our comprehension. Our atoms will be recycled, either to an inert substance or possibly to the plant or animal kingdom. You are too important just to disintegrate, melt and dissolve back to nature and be forgotten. Our spirit is eternal. Our choice for the soul is either heaven or hell. Don't allow self, Satan or world influence to prohibit or restrict your potential for the most important love relationship of your remaining short life. God loves me with an unconditional "Agape" love. There is no greater love to experience. Who would die on a cross for you? God gives my heartfelt **belief** in Jesus as the only answer to our standing in the cosmic apologetic revelation sequence. We are made of atoms including a unique spirit which we can convert from self domination as found in all other animal forms, to Jesus as Lord through a heartfelt belief in the gospel.

As previously discussed, to receive full benefit of the light of the gospel, we must position ourselves for maximum light exposure. The greater the light exposure, the healthier the plant, greater growth, and abundant fruit production. The more we feed and protect our roots of Christian apologetics, the deeper they penetrate into our core, the stronger and more difficult to extract. As a plant seeks the electromagnetic energy of light for survival, so we are destined following belief to seek spiritual light for spiritual survival and growth by a close walk with Jesus through the Word, Holy Spirit and prayer. Obedience and diligence, with our backs turned on sin and hypocrisy.

I must be driven by belief, not feelings. God's love is not dependent upon feelings but by a heartfelt belief and trust in the gospel truth. Look at the Creator, not what I envision, but what he envisions. I want my soul to be changed, transformed by utilizing the God-given cerebral cortex with construction and expression for all my thoughts. Not dominated by the subconscious or lower brainstem reflex mechanism. The seed of belief is a gift from God, the beginning of metamorphosis and sanctification to flush a corrupt soul. This is preparation for conversion and eventual companionship with Jesus for the soul following our physical death. Preparation of our soul for eternity with the Creator. Seek ways to improve spiritual health today. Soul health promotes physical health by a strong reinforced belief in the gospel and experiencing God's love and presence. John 10:10, "I am come that they have life, and that they may have it more abundantly."

This improvement to physical health can be objectively measured by the elevated serum blood levels of the hormonal neurotransmitters. Strengthen the soul through a habit to visualize the cross, God's forgiveness, the open veil, God's love and his omnipresence, the Holy Spirit. Does my soul, character, express Christ with words and actions? What did I do today that only a Christian would do? To how many people a day for 30 years do you think Paul spoke of the risen Christ? Yes, my words and actions must be expressed from belief and not temporal feelings of the lower brainstem. The ethos I desire is a reflection from my belief; whatever is true, noble, pure, right, admirable, lovely, excellent or praiseworthy. To be as conclusive and profound as the blast from a canon. A gentle yet profound blast that results in a lasting impression.

This is only possible through the constant employment with no lag time or time off, and full working order of God's thought filter of Philippians 4:8, yielding to the guidance of the Holy Spirit. The health of the soul is seen in your character and behavior. A healthy soul is filled every day with the apologetics of the reassurance of God's presence and love for you. Do not contaminate with self, Satan or world influence. Spiritual health is a compliment to physical health, interrelated as discussed. The neurotransmitters play an integral role in determining the level of our psychological and physiological well-being which are positively influenced by the awareness and meditation on God's love. I must awaken every morning with belief in God's love and express thankfulness, reinforced through apologetics, and fall asleep every night with the same thoughts of God's love with thankfulness in my heart. Be in the habit of replacing all negative thoughts. Jesus is Lord. It is easy to fall away from visualizing the cross and what it means to me. Be diligent. God's love, the Holy Spirit's presence, and eternity should be foremost in my thoughts, replacing counterproductive thoughts that bombard us daily.

It is not creation that should awe us but the Creator. My misdirection early in life was the focus of attention and awe on creation and not the Creator. This was for many years a setback for me. When I see something beautiful of creation, I should thank the Creator openly, multiple times daily. With scientific study the tendency and inclination is to be led astray with the workings, diversity, interrelationships and function of the creation and not on the Creator. Awe should be reserved for the Creator, not scientific events. Everything is dependent upon belief and apologetics for motivation to believe in God's personal love. All is dependent upon the seed of belief, to be implanted into our soul. The gospel promises have a major impact on our health status. If my soul is filled every morning with apologetic truths and love, both soul and body benefit. No fear, no guilt, God's presence whether we feel it or not, heaven and eternal security. No reason for us to be overcome or dominated by limitations from self, Satan or world. Be confident, walk erect with shoulders back and always be thankful.

What are the immediate benefits of belief?

☐ Spiritual security with confidence in eternity.

☐ Cleansing and rebirth to the soul.

☐ Confidence in the indwelling presence of the Holy Spirit.

☐ A physiological and psychological benefit from an ongoing increase in the production of vital neurohormones.

☐ A restored self image as God intended, based on the awareness of his love and adoption.

Most people avoid suggestions of known and scientifically established ways to improve physical health desiring rather to retain unhealthy habits. They may respond to your advice for a limited time but invariably revert back to their unhealthy habits. How can we expect them to be concerned about the health of their souls that they cannot even see? Most people have to be in the ICU before appreciating a life saving medical cure. It will be too late if they are on the way to hell to save their souls. The only way to spiritually motivate is that they understand the eternal fate of their sin-filled, self-focused soul. Our soul is eternal. Destination, heaven or hell, saved or lost, a rotting corpse or a rebirth.

What do you believe occurs after death? We have to believe something. The question opens all doors from Christian, cultic, and to all secular fabrications. Most cultures have historically devised cultic avenues seeking to satisfy the implanted God quest. Dominant are idols and bondage to satanic controlled beliefs. What is the process to change our human nature instincts in order to experience a Christ-centered rebirth in our inbred quest for God?

1. We must immediately recognize the eternal significance of our totally corrupt soul, destined for hell.
2. Our understanding and belief in the authenticity and historical truth of Jesus to his identity as the God of the cosmos.
3. The miracle of new birth is dependent upon belief and total surrender to the lordship of Jesus. Understanding of his complete forgiveness of past, present and future sins through belief and a bonded trust of dependency upon the Holy Spirit.

A progressive sanctification (set apart to become holy) from the seed of belief deposited in our souls.

4. Faith follows belief and repentance. **Faith breeds hope.** Trust in the gospel is a gift from God.

5. A new life in Christ, seeking to follow our repentant thought reprogramming with the Beatitudes and believe that God has a place for us in heaven.

6. If we believe change in our spiritual nature is possible through God, then we should be able to believe God can perform a change in our physical health. Yes, this can be objectively measured by the serum blood levels of neurotransmitters that facilitate physiological and psychological well-being, levels augmented directly by the awareness and appreciation of God's love on a personal basis.

The desire and access of this God-given inborn spiritual/physiological gift should dominate our daily thoughts to focus on God's love. A proven cure prescribed, but must be taken daily.

Revelation 3:20, The Kingdom of God is the presence of the Holy Spirit and the totality of more to come. What we see and what we do not see in the future. You can only see the future if Jesus is Lord now in your heart. God is King now and in the future. I want my spiritual desires to be as tenacious and diligent as a root unrelentingly seeking a water source so intently deliberate so as to be disruptive to my base behavior. I should be as diligent with spiritual health pursuits as I am with physical health concerns. Each of these seven apologetic items point and include evidence of God's love for me. With Biblically based apologetics, be ready to explain the reason for the hope that you have.

1. The entire physical and life abundant creation is evidence at this moment of God's presence.

2. Conscience is evidence of our need for God due to his implantation within us the awareness of moral behavioral limits and parameters that we find difficult to live by.

3. The scriptures, God's plan written over 1500 years by 40 different authors, his redemptive purpose and plan.

4. Jesus as our redeemer, the incarnation of God. "he who has seen me has seen the Father." Either he was crazy or this is a valid statement.

5. The gospel pointing to "the small gate and the narrow way that leadeth" to heaven dependent on faith in Jesus as Lord, Matthew 7:14.

6. The influence of apologetic truth on our brain promotes peace and physiological homeostasis including healthy brain hormone secretions augmented and facilitated by our constant recall and assurance of God's love for us, verified by biochemical research. This is a big deal if we desire the optimum well-being of physiological and psychological health and should be in our thoughts throughout the day.

7. Acceptance of God's love in our inner being, the Holy Spirit, which is God's appointed antidote to fear, insecurity, hopelessness, anguish and all negative poisoned arrows from self, Satan and the world.

My hope for eternal life is dependent upon the resurrection of Christ. Does my behavior reflect this? God's love, awareness and presence, is only experienced if we are plugged into the heartfelt belief of the gospel. We are extremely complex in anatomy and physiology. It had to take a God who is responsible for the universe to design and create us. It is fantasy to think this was possible without an intelligent designer. If God made the universe with us in mind as a creature with a spirit, I should be in contact with prayer, as God is spirit. "Don't be anxious, but with prayer, supplication and thanksgiving make your requests known to God and the peace of God that transcends all human understanding will guard our hearts, minds and thoughts in Christ Jesus." Philippians 4: 6-7.

Jesus came as a Redeemer to dispel fear, provide hope, forgive man as sinners and for personal fellowship now and for eternity. This is dependent upon belief. We are slow to accept the gospel due to the dominance of our "I" problem from early childhood. All conditioning from birth was 100% for self satisfaction. No emphasis on Jesus as Lord. Childhood pleasures, adult pleasures, old age pleasures, are all vanity. The quality and quantity of joys to be anticipated in eternity cannot be predicted, described, or imagined. How can we enjoy heaven with our focus now only on self? Prayer was a priority to Jesus. This should also be a priority to me. To pray is not a task or just a quick response but to pray with the purpose to communicate with God, a joyful desire to have a personal relationship. A joyous visit with the one who loves you and knows every cell, marrow and fiber in your body. Psalm 139. How often did I desire to communicate with my first love? Psalm 16:11, "In thy presence is fullness of joy". It is best for children to hear from early childhood, "Jesus is Lord," as this has been proven to reinforce a beneficial dominant habit of thought. It is absolutely necessary to abort our "I" problem. We are encouraged by Jesus to daily carry our cross of death to self, to the cross of redemption. Therefore only by the Holy Spirit can we abort our "I" problem of dominant self focus as the icon of our worship. The Holy Spirit must reign and be in command of our thoughts, Jesus is Lord.

If my thoughts are dominated with self-saturated "feelings", Satan or world influence, the end result is temporal with a self-limited endpoint. Full of negative spiritual unhealthy thoughts. If on the other hand with Jesus as Lord, our thoughts will have an eternal endpoint. Overcome the influence of self, flesh, Satan, world and plug with belief into the awaiting socket of God's love, the Holy Spirit desiring to be admitted at your request for love and fellowship. Our mental health is influenced by hormones secreted by the brain. A heartfelt presence of the Holy Spirit and enjoying God's love facilitates secretion of these valuable hormones; dopamine, oxytocin, and serotonin. A marked reduction of these hormones is found with constant stress which is counterproductive to a healthy mental and physiological state.

Override this with a dominant belief, resting on God's love. This is the secret for stress replacement, meditating on God's love for you. Considerable pharmaceutical search for the ideal antidepressant has revealed our neurohormone oxytocin to spike in many activities related to love related experiences. During times of affection between mother and child, sexual satisfaction between adults, interestingly, studies between pet owners and their canine partners revealed spikes in oxytocin merely following periods of peering into each other's eyes.

Levels were elevated in both canine and owner. It would be interesting to view a graph of a person's past and present timeline to the production output of oxytocin and add in the factor of subjective well-being. It is quite evident that we are healthier and happier individuals in the presence of experiencing a one-on-one love relationship. We are all beggars looking for love. Therefore to experience an oxytocin level that will evoke the feeling of irrevocable well-being I must live in the daily reality with a dominant one-on-one intimate love relationship with my devoted Sherpa mountain guide Paraclete, the Holy Spirit. In addition to mental health, cardiovascular health is also dependent upon a complex relationship with oxytocin and of course neurohormones control the level of our total health status. We must deal stress a spiritual cure.

Live in a state of God's love felt in your heart, and a response to love for God first and neighbor second. A sure cure to constant stress and negative thoughts. Philippians 4:6-7. Don't be anxious, pray with thanksgiving and experience God's peace. Don't allow Satan to have a foot in the door of God's love. Satan desires to override our awareness of God's love with doubt, fears and self-deprecation, a negative self image. The state of our mind is either positive or negative and rarely neutral. The antidote for negative thought is the heartfelt presence of God's love. Your dominant thought and vision of Christ on the cross for **YOU** will override all negative thoughts. Admit to God's love for you moment by moment, as a habit, based on apologetic thought. A direct line to the creator of the cosmos through Jesus Christ. If in doubt or depressed, be an overcomer., only possible with a heart filled presence of the Holy Spirit and God's love. Our encouragement of neurohormone production is as critical to our level of well-being as a life saving transthoracic intracardiac injection of adrenalin at the time of a cardiac arrest.

God gave humans self-will and spirit to determine thoughts and communication. Self, world, and Satan should not determine our thoughts, but "take captive all thoughts to the obedience of Christ," 2nd Corinthians 10:5. Filter all thoughts with "whatever is true, honorable, right, pure, lovely, admirable, excellent and worthy of praise before speaking or actions." Philippians 4:8. A must, not optional, otherwise I am lower brainstem dependent, shallow and self-centered, a spiritually fatal existence now for the precious short time we have left in this life and a fatal eternal prognosis.

Prayer and knowing God's love for us in our hearts, mind and the presence of the Holy Spirit is the antidote to depression, fear, guilt and hopelessness. Dependent upon a heartfelt belief. He made the universe and created life with atoms and with humans included soul and spirit. Avoid all negative thought if you want homeostasis and peace. "Don't be anxious about anything but with prayer, supplication and thankfulness, make your requests known to God and the peace of God that transcends all human understanding will guard your hearts, minds and thoughts in Christ Jesus." Philippians 4:6-7. Luke 10:27, "Love the Lord with all your heart, soul, strength, mind and love your neighbor as yourself." We can only successfully live the Christian life in the presence of the Holy Spirit. Defeat if we fall back on self. Must totally surrender to the Lordship of Christ, no other option if we desire to win the spiritual battle. Don't live perched, unstable on the spiritual fence as the majority who claim and check off Christianity as their faith of preference on a form of inquiry. But rather, in the daily presence and open arms of the Holy Spirit following total surrender to Jesus as

Lord.

Apologetics open the door to an understanding and a solid spiritual belief of "hold-fast" strength, securely attached with either calm seas or storms raging above. God's love for us is found in each apologetic point and directs me to the Beatitudes. God first and neighbor second. Maintain a habit of enjoying the presence of the Holy Spirit and ask every morning for a refill based upon belief. Paul taught in Ephesians that all believers are sealed with the Spirit when they believe, Ephesians 4:30; 1:13-14, but not all are filled, since this depends on yieldedness to God's will. Maintain a full tank, clean out and empty all the debris. Fill with joy, courage, spirituality and Christian character. Psychological peace is based on the right perspective of the Holy Spirit and of eternity in our hearts. Jesus as Lord. Fix your eyes to Heaven's glory.

Will God's love help you take every thought captive to the obedience of Christ? Answer, it's how we respect the importance of God's love for us. It must be a habit. To capture and filter all thoughts, pause and count to five. Do I value God's love over all temporal thoughts from self, world, Satan or material idols? God's love is represented by the cross. We must believe and visualize to receive. Do I see the split open veil, representing our access to God through my fidelity to the Lordship of Jesus Christ? Do I experience total forgiveness through the words of Christ on the cross, "It is finished"? Don't fight to stay afloat in a sea of remorse but relax and reflect on God's love, the only eternally approved and certified life saving flotation device, saving lives for eternity for over 4000 years, since recorded in the book of Job. What is the most important issue in my life? A personal Christ relationship and eternal life, all starts with apologetics which yields and reinforces the core of belief. A strong apologetic belief core results in strong faith. Contrast this to a weak belief, which results in little or no faith. Faith is measured by our actions.

Does my behavior reflect faith in Jesus? Do I have a passion for the lost souls that I'm in contact with daily? Reach out and plant seeds. We cannot always expect a ripe reception. Parable of the sower, Matthew 13:1-23. However we are expected to sow seeds in all seasons and soils regardless of anticipated soil receptivity. Jesus ate with, and taught sinners and tax collectors, Matthew 9:10. "Healthy people don't need a doctor, sick people do," Matthew 9:12. However in Matthew 7:6, Jesus states "not to cast pearls to swine," that is, we are to share the gospel but if not welcome, to move on, "shake the dust off your feet and leave," Matthew 10:14. We are not responsible for the soil quality of people's hearts at that moment. Jesus describes the various types of soils to expect. As seeds deposited beside the road and eaten by birds, rocky places with no depth of soil, soil filled with thorns that choked out the seeds. Finally good soil, yielding multiples of crop. Matthew 11:15, "He who has ears, let him hear."

My hope is based on the resurrection. Think apologetics when you view the resurrection. The first report was by Mary Magdalene and would not have been documented unless factual, as females were considered unreliable and of questionable credibility. The apostles lives dramatically changed from fear to proclamation. Alexander and Rufus, the sons of Simon of Cyrene were active in the church as a result of their father's testimony to the resurrection. Mark 15:21. What are the now and future rewards of belief in Christ? A glorious hope for the future, based on his resurrection. His love, the presence of the Holy

Spirit is the antidote to fear, guilt, hopelessness, and is to be experienced today. The God of love is my belief. Jesus on the cross. The God who made the stars preferred to suffer pain and death than live without you. John 3:17.

Apologetic confidence in a personal relationship with the God of the cosmos yields a tangible and palpable reward by reinforcing belief and motivates me to stay plugged into the socket of God's love. I need to experience a tangible reward for the strong habit of apologetic thought. The reward is peace of mind, hope, and identification with the ongoing presence of Jesus, Holy Spirit, to know his love now and a down-payment for eternity. We should not have to force a habit of thought but think of the enjoyment of the reward of these thoughts in contrast to the rewards of my current thoughts. How much of my day is spent on pondering edifying thoughts from the upper brain centers that will bless, to the time wasted on negative and fearful thoughts. I should live in a state of constant enjoyment and thanksgiving based upon a foundation of apologetics. Peace of mind, eternal hope and the presence of the belief in God's love. God's love should be as real as a "drive by" presence, be thankful for this moment of faith. Romans 15:13, "may the God of hope fill you with all joy and peace in trusting him, that you will abound in hope, through the power of the Holy Spirit." We must stay plugged into the socket of God's love. As a metaphor of the Trinity, the three-pronged heavy duty marine socket to twist and lock for a permanent connection, designed to be not waterproof but a sin-proof connection.

Always available, the love of God awaits my heartfelt plug of belief from apologetics. A gift from God. I must have a valid trust and belief in Jesus Christ. Without this heartfelt belief, I cannot plug into

God's waiting love.

"Sanctify Christ as Lord in your heart and always be ready to give an answer for the hope you have in you, yet with gentleness and reverence." 1st Peter 3:15. If apologetics are true, then the gospel is true and his love for me depending upon my belief, is the antidote to all fear, anxiety, hopelessness, guilt and I can rest on the belief of eternal life. When Jesus came, the world was dominated by fear, superstition, hopelessness, worship of idols, "mystery religions" based upon "works" and secularized Judaism. Conversion to Jesus as Lord is a gift based upon belief, the beginning of a soul metamorphosis, the reward at death, that my soul will be with Jesus. Experience now the joy of the process within the chrysalis of my soul, of sanctification, resulting from the precious seed of belief. Feel the fetal movements of regeneration, new birth, the mystery of rebirth and love within the chrysalis of my soul. I can only experience God's love if I have a strong comprehensive apologetic statement and core to Jesus as Lord.

Most people do not have a grasp on the now rewards of belief in Christ. We must have a foundation of repentance and belief to be right with God. This must start with a strong apologetic statement which includes the reality and purpose of Christ. The availability of his Lordship and love, fellowship through prayer, reading God's word, and a resulting peace that transcends all human understanding. Belief in God's love, the Holy Spirit, should block any doubt from our soul, conscience or subconscious. When we plug a heartfelt belief into the love socket we receive confidence to overcome all poison-tipped arrows attacking our soul, the result of fulfilling the command to put on the full armor of God, Ephesians 6:11-18. "Do not be anxious, pray with supplication and thanksgiving making your requests known to

God and the peace of God that transcends all human understanding will guard your hearts, minds and thoughts in Christ Jesus." Philippians 4:6-7. Joy, the outward expression of inward spiritual confidence of God's love, should be my trademark. My trademark of joy should be experienced as an exclamation mark and not a question mark of doubt.

The most motivating and threatening emotions with humans has always been and always will be fear, guilt and superstition. Belief in God's presence, the Holy Spirit and his love is the antidote that will completely erase these negative thoughts, quantified by the strength of our belief. I am in contact with the Creator of the universe through general and specific revelation. This reveals Jesus Christ as our intermediary to God. When my mind wanders to self-centeredness and self-gratification, Satan or world influence, the result is worry, hopelessness, guilt, and a self-limited end-point. Galatians 5:19. The proven cure is to think of the Creator of the universe and to give thanksgiving multiple times a day for the evidence of God's presence, his love for me and that I am able to communicate my concerns. Those who experience confidence are firmly plugged into belief and live "real time" in his presence.

Start daily with thoughts of the Creator of the universe including all life. God relates to each individual through Jesus Christ. Do I see evidence of God through creation, conscience, gospel and God's word? Belief is an action verb and it's expression is dependent upon my overcoming self, Satan, world influence and plugging directly with my three pronged Trinitarian plug of belief into the awaiting socket of God's love. God's love is the waiting reward for a valid true heartfelt belief in Jesus and the cross. Revelation 3:20, The Prodigal Son, and John 3:16, Ephesians 3:17-19.

Live with the habit as an overcomer. of self, Satan, and world influence. By this, to experience a constant fellowship with God through prayer should be my number one goal with eternal life as a promised expectation. The most important goal is my daily ongoing relationship. Do I really fellowship with God through the Holy Spirit or am I in bondage as a fool to self and a dominant lower brainstem existence? Jesus came down the ladder to reach me. I did not have to climb up the ladder with a perfect profile of righteousness. He is always there. Live as an overcomer not controlled by the worm of sin and hypocrisy that lives in my apple. If God designed and made the cosmos, he very well designed and made us with the same atoms as all other life forms. There are two unique components that God gave to human life and not to other forms of life. As humans are unique with a soul and spirit. When we die a physical death, our atoms are recycled. Our soul will live for eternity as a result of sanctification from the seed of belief with new thought priorities and a new mindset of conversion. Romans 12:1-2, "I urge you therefore, brethren by the mercies of God to present your bodies a living and holy sacrifice acceptable to God which is your spiritual service of worship. And do not be conformed to this world, but be transformed by the renewing of your mind, that you may prove what the will of God is, that which is good and acceptable and perfect." There is no second chance. Luke 16, the story of the rich man and Lazarus. Repent now, for the Kingdom of God is near, Jesus is Lord now, which is all important to our daily thought. The seed of belief must enjoy metamorphosis and sanctification now before physical death. In the absence of a new birth and conversion, then at the time of physical death our soul departs to Hades with no second chance.

Our soul harbors who we are, our character, the sum total of all prior deposits as a storage chamber. Our spirit is designed by God for communication on a spiritual level. Our atoms are recycled back to nature at death, however the spirit is eternal, with final destination either heaven or hell. Our spirits dictate how we think and how we metabolize spiritual knowledge and information. There will be no change in us unless there is total surrender to Jesus as Lord. No partial or vacillating surrender. Repent through a Beatitude soul transformation and trust in God's love for you and the Holy Spirit's presence, enjoyed through frequent prayer. A heartfelt God's love must dominate all thoughts and decisions.

The apostles were under total surrender to the Lordship of Christ at his final departure and anticipated his return. The apostles had the Holy Spirit in their hearts and the recent image of Christ in their minds thus, he was very real to them. The Kingdom of God is now, following a personal total surrender to Christ, and the Kingdom of God is in the future, when Christ returns. The Kingdom of God by definition is the authority and rule of a king, so the Kingdom of God means a rule or reign of God. We will be healed in heaven. The Kingdom of God is experienced within ourselves now following total surrender of self, to Jesus as Lord, the Holy Spirit. We are expected to carry our cross at all times. As we know too well, it is easy to lay aside or drop and return to self as God. Carrying our cross is death to self and identifying with Jesus.

Two ways to know someone, to know about, or to really know someone. We must experience God's presence to really know him, like knowing a distant location. We must have a personal experience with that location for confidence, I have been there. I know the area. Not just to know about the location. We can say that we know about someone or that we know the person intimately. Apologetics give overwhelming evidence to be able to know God intimately as a result of our belief in Christ and his love for us, the cross. This belief and trust in Jesus is a gift from God, following our epiphany from apologetics of the divinity of Christ. With the question, do I know God, the basis of our belief is a strong apologetic statement. God made the universe and designed us with soul and spirit to communicate. Wash away self, Satan and world influence to experience God's peace. I must be an overcomer. Constantly I need to encourage my faith by worshiping God and reading his word. Do not be double-minded, James 1:8, have a healthy eye, Matthew 6:22. To know God is to desire to think like Jesus, Beatitude thinking. Matthew 5:3-11.

God's design is for us to become spiritually alive by belief, Jesus as Lord followed with metamorphosis, sanctification in our souls, a rebirth in our souls. As a result we will not experience the second death at judgment, our souls will be permanently with Jesus. Unless I believe Jesus as Lord, I am spiritually dead. We need to be totally surrendered to God. It is too common that the Christian faith has been over-intellectualized, reducing much of it to the level of words and propositions. Knowing God has become little more than statements about God, a cosmetic religiosity with no remission of sins. "Thank him for all he has done, then you will experience God's peace that transcends all human understanding. His love will guard our hearts, minds, and thoughts as you live in Christ Jesus." Discover daily pleasure and peace by listening and obeying his transcendent voice. God calls us to love him "with all our heart, mind, soul and strength and to love your neighbor as yourself." Luke 10:27, Matthew 22:37.

It is not trying harder but character, to bend our minds and to change our thought paradigm to those of the Beatitudes, as we so desire to repent and restore our soul. Matthew 5:3-12.

1. To be poor in spirit, is to be humble and aware of the final eternal destination of our corrupt souls.

2. To mourn is to mourn over our sins and failures as well as those of others.

3. Humble and meek does not translate to a personality of meekness but refers to confidence in Jesus and his teachings and instructions.

4. To hunger and thirst for righteousness refers to the dominating desire for right thinking and to control thoughts prior to sensory receptor responses.

5. Mercy, show mercy to others as God shows mercy to us.

6. Pure hearts, holiness, "for only the holy will see God." Hebrews 12:14. Only on the gangplank of faith and repentance can one access the ship of holiness.

7. Peacemakers, Philippians 4:6-7, a verse of habit as we must have peace with God before we have the capacity or ability to profile a valid peace.

8. Persecuted for righteousness, persecution authenticates your position in Christ Jesus. We cannot be indifferent about Jesus Christ.

Do I value the lordship of Christ daily in my life as experiencing the Kingdom of God, with God, the Holy Spirit ruling? Explain the love of God with your readiness to explain apologetics as the first step to understanding the hope in one's life. The God of creation is a God with whom I can personally relate and communicate.

Otherwise I'm the one with my head buried in the sand or with blinders still covering my eyes. Where do I need to improve my thoughts and achievements with each Beatitude? Do I recall daily each one and where I can improve? This is completely a 180° aberrancy from natural man. This change in behavior is a component of our repentance. Only with the reminder of apologetics, and to plug into God's love will I be motivated to be dominated by Beatitude thinking for a real soul transformation. The common denominator with the Beatitudes is to be directed away from a life of self-centeredness to a paradigm of God first and neighbor second. Do I value the lordship of Christ daily in my life, for only with this desire will I live the Beatitudes. How do I express God first? Reject my immediate sensory receptor natural reflexes of the lower brainstem and instead translate all thoughts in the cerebral cortex prior to expression. God's Kingdom will only be experienced if I live the Beatitudes, Jesus as Lord, God first, neighbor second. This is only possible with the help of the Holy Spirit and personal diligence as I must daily experience a complete and total surrender to Jesus as Lord.

People with guilt and fears expose themselves through compensatory personality disorders, recognized by abnormal appearance, overt strange or withdrawn behavior. Either way they are easy to recognize. Multitudes hide their conflicts behind masks. We do not see the person but a self protective mask hiding hypocrisy. A shiny healthy appearing apple. In fact, all people hide themselves behind a mask of acceptability, not revealing their true self. Those who seek psychiatric help usually are seeking approval to continue in their falsely satisfying proclivities, habits and misbehavior. The majority of people in our society seek secular answers to guilt and fear through personality or unusual physical appearance, aberrations of behavior, idols, drugs or sexual deviations.

A simple, single encouragement may have lasting effect for years to a person. Look for opportunities to give encouragement. Example, respect and complement positive traits and achievements of people. Show that you respect and admire their positive points and tell people you love them. People will try to reach the level of your expectation, however their motivation is diminished when they consider your own personal failures as a judge and encourager either perceived or documented. It is best to be encouraged from one of known pure and transparent character. Our actions speak louder than words. Everyone has a hurt. Maybe a person is hurting and needs genuine sympathy. The same experience with God, if you are truly plugged into belief and God's love, you will be encouraged and motivated to excel to His expectations.

If a person lives with constant negative exposure and criticism, it is not unexpected that physiological or psychological ill health will eventually be manifested, the result of the suppression of our hormonal neurotransmitters. Encouragement is so important to ourselves and others for success in preventative medicine. Ever present negative mental fears and burdens can strip a person from experiencing God's love. It is very important to tell people you love them in Christ, actively allowing the Holy Spirit to flow through you, it is not I, but the Holy Spirit. Look at people as God sees them, not through your eyes of fixed prejudice. People are swallowed with guilt in their conscious and hidden subconscious level, in need of reassurance from a respected judge or friend. People are suffering in spite of their quiet pretense. Important is eye contact, confidence, shoulders back, erect stature, diligence, strong apologetics, sympathy, transparency, a genuine smile from the joy of the Lord yields untold benefits, both to the recipient as well as to the provider, all guiding me to encourage people to express their concerns. People do not care how much you know until they know how much you care.

Explain to people the psychological and physiological benefits of living in the awareness of God's love for them. You may be casting seeds that will germinate with beautiful lasting dividends to that person. Don't pass up the opportunity. Begin today, for your efforts will be rewarded. Indeed, what have I done today that only a Christian would do?

Available to our sinful and corrupt soul, we are given the opportunity to respond to his presence and love. We either accept or reject Jesus as Lord, as God offers his love to all sinners. A true heartfelt belief will be followed by repentance. We are not required to first climb the ladder carrying righteousness to win God's acceptance. He came down to our level to offer the seed of belief to our souls of total corruption. If we recognize the rotten status and mortal bleeding wounds of our soul and seriously consider its eternal unrepentant destination, we will desire restoration, a rebirth, the result of planting the eternity packed seed of belief into our souls.

If we really experience a heartfelt belief in the historical reality of Jesus than we must thus believe in God's cosmic plan for us. We cannot prove scientifically but we are certain of God's omnipresence as confirmed in scriptures, logic and reason and experienced through the epiphany of realizing that there must be a cosmic controlling God. God is always there, his presence may not be felt as in the case of Job but he is always with us. What Job needed was not theology but sympathy, not condemnation but affirmation, with compassion. Painful wounds call for love, understanding and healing. Certainly everyone has painful wounds, mental and physical that need healing, as did Job. When someone goes through a trial or tribulation, he feels a sense of guilt, does not need Job's encouraging friends, Satan. He needs to be reminded of God's love based upon trust in Christ. We do not need criticism or lectures when we are down nor a reinforcement of self condemnation, we need encouragement.

We need sincere sympathy, warm compassion from trust in God's love and omnipresence. An open wound needs tender loving care, wound care for healing, and time. The best response is the result of the "Best Physician." Ask people what is most troubling to them at this time. Do not look down on people, no one is without issues. We need to remember the path our own moccasins have trod. We may see weaknesses in a person's appearance or awkward behavior, but never by your action reinforce their negative self opinions. Always look for ways to offer encouragement from a level of non-entrapment or judgment.

It is so easy to pick up on your rejection, as they are expecting this affect from you. Do not overreact with false and insincere approval. Give a person a way out when discussing sensitive issues. Approach them as you would a wounded, fearful animal and beware to not make them feel that they are being cornered without an escape. People will try to reinforce their negative self image by baiting you to agree or show agreement with their poor negative self image. They expect you to show signs of your first impression in agreement to their negative self image, to which they are accustomed in social situations. Do not be tricked into this, as you must avoid the trap of their negative reinforcement and hopelessness.

God's love, Jesus on the cross, will never be experienced unless you experience in your heart the historic apologetic truth of the suffering of Jesus on the cross for you. It does us well to firmly imprint this picture in our minds eye of what Christ did voluntarily for each of us. Christ teaches us through the substrate of his foundational teachings, God first and neighbor second, not "me" first. This Beatitude thinking must dominate my thoughts if I desire new righteously orientated dominant neural pathways. This is the path to repentance. God's love is a doorbell after we are plugged into belief in the gospel, to open the door for fellowship with Jesus, the Holy Spirit. Revelation 3:20. With our three pronged plug of Trinitarian belief be ready for the awaiting socket of God's love, his knocking at the door of our heart.

"GOD'S GIFT OF HIS COMFORTING AGAPE LOVE IS OUR GREATEST TREASURE AND SOURCE OF ENCOURAGEMENT, HOPE, AND THE ANTIDOTE TO DEPRESSION, FEAR, LONELINESS, PESSIMISM. THE ANSWER TO THE CRY OF EVERY SOUL."

We believe in the historic reality of Jesus, this results in a heartfelt belief in God's cosmic plan for us, an epiphanous gift from God. Ephesians 2:10, "For we are his workmanship, created in Christ Jesus for good works, which God prepared beforehand, that we should walk in them." Only possible if we are filled with the Holy Spirit. Jesus removed the blinders from our eyes and we see the truth of the gospel and Jesus' relationship with the revelation of general and specific apologetics. With this seed of belief deposited into our soul the true miracle of a spiritual metamorphosis occurs with the goal of sanctification, conversion, a new birth. The seed of belief deposited in our soul is nourished with our awareness of God's love. If no awareness of God's love than death to the seed of belief. A valid heartfelt belief must be seen if a person claims to be a Christian. "Your actions are so loud that I cannot hear what you say." Must unite a heartfelt belief to God's waiting love to produce a behavioral change. So lacking in the "Christian" society today. Total surrender to Christ is lacking. Our claims of belief and God's love are valueless and a fraud without a behavioral change. Starts with the way we think, the Beatitudes and 2nd. Timothy 1:7, "For God has not given us a spirit of timidity, but of power, and love and discipline." Translated, God has not given us a spirit of "fear, cowardice or defeat," but of "unlimited power, all hell tried to hold Jesus on the cross," and love "God's agape, unconditional love, not our shallow love," and "sound judgment, self control."

"Do not be anxious about anything, pray with true thankfulness, with supplication make your requests known to God, experience the peace of God that transcends all human understanding that guards our hearts, thoughts and minds in Christ Jesus."

Philippians 4:6-7. A peace free of ulterior motives and hypocrisy is a peace that encourages thoughts; true, noble, right, pure, lovely, admirable, excellent and praiseworthy.

The hypocrite on the other hand lives with hidden evil motives in his heart experienced as an undulating, curling, expanding, contracting, coiling, intestinal parasitic worm enjoying the dark, sucking the life blood with no rest for the host as the worm serves and provides for himself, draining the soul of strength and reserve. In the absence of total commitment and the Holy Spirit, our life is strictly self-serving, supporting this ubiquitous worm. My description a result of one year postgraduate research in parasitology, Allan Hancock Foundation, USC, prior to medical school. Our thought filter of Philippines 4:8 is nonexistent for righteous expression. All humans possess this tenacious worm of hypocrisy that has learned to thrive and multiply in the absence of a complete and valid Christ commitment. Psalm 119:11, "Thy word have I have hid in mine heart that I might not sin against thee." Psalm 119:105, "Thy word is a lamp unto my feet, and a light unto my path." God's word in our heart and total commitment is the antidote and cure to the presence of hypocrisy that haunts and devours our souls.

In discussing this issue of how to deal with hypocrisy with an older theologian of notable stature, he stated that he personally finds solace and comfort to avoid hypocrisy by opening his Bible with greater frequency, Scripture memory, rumination, memorization, prayer and application. He related the story of Elisha in 2nd. Kings 4:38-41 when Elisha added "flour" (God's word) as an antidote to the poisoned stew that contained various fruits and herbs of the world, which was than safely eaten; replacement therapy with God's word. I was not surprised to hear from this gentleman that his approach to overcome hypocritical inclinations is a habit of using with diligence God's intended cure for all believers. The Word. Use the "good eye" of Matthew 6:22 and not be a "double-minded man, unstable in all our ways." James 1:8.

As humans we will never eradicate hypocrisy this side of heaven. We can only hope to suppress the symptoms with the prescribed replacement, our diligence to the presence of Biblical and Holy Spirit dependency. Jesus hates hypocrisy and was very vocal as the gospels frequently have recorded. We all have cholesterol to varying levels as people differ metabolically. The expression of disease is experienced with elevated levels. Statin drugs will reduce the blood level as long as you take them, but if you stop, the levels return. You will never be "cured," but if you desire to reduce the risk of degenerative vascular disease from plaque deposits you will continue with the prescription. Not a definitive cure but a way to effectively manage the potential morbidity and mortality resulting from severe atherosclerosis.

We don't have to feel guilty with this hereditary "gift" of hypocrisy, just recognize and admit that it exists and stay diligent in following the advice of the "Best Physician." How to be fun to live with? The stronger our beliefs based on Scripture, the lesser chance of responding with compromising temporal sensory feelings that we may regret if expressed. We desire our thoughts strong with Scripture and perseverance utilizing the thought filter of Philippines 4:8. Only if hope, joy and peace dominate our thoughts will we be fun to live with. Paul gives the Biblical source for us to fix in our minds with several Scriptures beginning with Romans 15:4, "For whatever was written in earlier times was written for our instruction, that through **perseverance** and **encouragement** of the **Scriptures** we might have **hope**." Again, Romans 15:12, Isaiah 11:10, "And again Isaiah says, " There shall come the root of Jesse, And He who arises to rule over the Gentiles, In Him shall the Gentiles **hope**." Jesus. Paul further states in his famous verse of encouragement, Romans 15:13, "Now may the God of **hope** fill you with all **joy** and **peace** in believing, that you will abound in **hope** by the power of the Holy Spirit." If we will be consistent in relying more on these Scriptures before responding and thus filled with hope, joy and peace, as my notable theologian friend in a prior paragraph gives as his personal cure, we will be a person fun to live with. Are you fun to live with? Yes, if filled with hope joy and peace. Does your cup "runneth over" with these healings?

If I am resting on feelings, let that rest be on God's love for me dependent upon my strong heartfelt belief in the gospel. God's love must be of greater influence and replacement than negative input from self, Satan and world. God's love represented by the cross is the most important influence to change our thoughts, words, behavior, habits, character and will positively influence healthy levels of our hormonal neurotransmitters for physiological and psychological well-being. If I believe this then I must wake up and live it, with strong habit.

Jesus told us to take up our cross and follow him daily. Translated, this is to die to self, the lower brainstem dominating our thoughts and behavior. The goal is total surrender to Jesus, an absolute must, before we can experience a metamorphosis from the seed of belief to progressive sanctification, identical as an embryo develops and maturates. If no total surrender, than as a developing fetus depends on the placenta; no placenta, no future. Your spiritual demise is guaranteed. God's undeserved love is the doorbell of Revelation 3:20. We must respond with whole heart, open the door of belief and plug into God's love, the Holy Spirit. This will be the antidote to all our fears of failure, guilt, corruption of soul, anxieties, anguish, and hopelessness, ending in despair. I want the presence of God's love to dominate and replace all negative thoughts. Atoms of our body at death are recycled. Spirit and soul are the open lines, our connection to God. Truly we are spiritual beings in an earth suit. Do I live as a spiritual being or just in an earth suit? If God rules over the universe, why should he not rule over me? This is the reason that God gave us a spirit for fellowship now. The major instruction is Jesus as Lord, not me. The goal is a spiritual relationship with Jesus, death to self, followed by a spiritual metamorphosis from the seed of belief. These changes of a new birth, metamorphosis, sanctification, conversion, must occur while we are still physically alive. If death occurs now while we are still spiritually dead there is no second chance. Our final fate is determined. Revelation 3:20, God's love and the Holy Spirit's presence in our hearts is the antidote to a life of fear, superstition, hopelessness, all dependent upon a strong heartfelt belief in Christ and the Gospel. Christianity is not a social fabric of human endeavor as are other religions, totally different. General and specific revelation apologetics reveal the existence of a living being who designed the cosmos and all life through a mechanism that our minds will never understand. This cosmic being, God, designed man with a brain totally different to all other animal forms; with soul and spirit included to be able to identify and communicate with our maker. We tend to look at other animal forms and see the similarities and identify with anthropomorphic comparisons when we really should be looking in the other direction and identifying our innate potential; as what does it mean that we "were made in the image of God," with self will and not totally dependent on the lower brainstem? Created by God for an adoption and to express the fruit of the spirit, through the implanted presence and submission to the Holy Spirit. I must not focus on the world for understanding but that of God's plan revealed through my epiphany from belief, faith and trust.

God first, not just felt in our minds as theory but must be felt in our hearts. This controls and determines how we think, our words, behavior, habits, soul, character and most important, our destiny. Cultivating the habit in thought of God first, provides an increase in confidence in our soul and character. Luke 18:40-43. Am I indebted to Christ as this blind man who now sees, or instead do I lack confidence of total forgiveness from the atonement of Christ on the cross? Is my love for Christ of partial incomplete surrender of the marginalized Christian lacking joy and peace? A marginalized Christian is a barren fruitless tree poised for the fire pit. Satan desires that we hear "partially finished" and not the beautiful words, "It is finished." Through faith we have been healed totally with complete forgiveness to enjoy the relationship of a loved adopted son.

Romans 5:1-2, "Therefore, since we have been justified through faith, we have peace with God through our Lord Jesus Christ, through whom we have gained access by faith into His grace in which we now stand. And we rejoice in the hope of the glory of God." My reward is to rest on the peak of Mount Everest (God's love) to view the entire world from this special appointed place, confident in being His son. Justified, expressing inexplicable exhilaration and joy from where he placed me at 29,000 feet. God desires that we live our lives from this vantage point of adoption. Romans 8:14, "For all those led by God's Spirit are God's sons." If Jesus died for me then no man is superior and I am equal in God's sight to all men on earth. A totally new identification with a new self image, as newly hatched eaglets protected beneath the spread wings of the mother eagle.

You can get the man out of the slum but you cannot get the slum out of the man, unless he is motivated by a heartfelt identification with a stronger neural engram of greater reward and truth; peace with God and His eternal presence, an adopted son. Rescued from a sea of debris and foul pollution. Christ is on record of never performing a partial healing. All complete and successful healings. I am now an adopted son, previously spiritually abandoned, lost and empty without hope. Am I currently enjoying the level of fellowship that I should be experiencing? It certainly is not God's fault. Romans 8:14-17 We are to no longer see ourselves as losers but with the now awakened spiritual alleles from the epiphany of belief in the historical authenticity of the life of Christ, we recognize that we are all equal members of Gods human colony. All formed with the same organs with only phenotype differences, yet the same offer of God's love. No one can claim superiority over another person. There is no appointed human, nor religious icon that deserves worship. We rejoice over this epiphany of all men created equal under God. By faith and the will of Christ we are totally healed mentally and spiritually and loved to a degree beyond imagination. To live in harmony with our maker for eternity. It is normal for a person walking by faith to experience exhilaration, other times it requires only the slightest knock to make one feel insecure and anxious. To counter this, we must be with a strong apologetic focus

124

and thought, reinforcing our personal existence to the God of the cosmos through our trust in Jesus Christ. Reinforce the heartfelt presence of God's love and 100% reassurance by a solid and unfaltering belief in the resurrection of Christ. Not just an intellectual acceptance but a moving experience in our hearts is daily required, including prayer. So much is dependent upon a strong apologetic persistent and recurrent recall to experience the peace of God with no anxiety, no worry. 1st. Thessalonians 5:16-18, "Rejoice always, pray without ceasing and be thankful in all circumstances for this is God's will for you in Christ Jesus." Reinforce your vulnerable walk by faith with a strong apologetic statement. That is: creation and the cosmos is the evidence of the omnipresence of God. Conscience, a DNA gene from God reveals our need for God to keep us on course. The most direct way to a destination is a straight line, avoid detours. The incarnation of Christ our redeemer and God's gift of His Word, the plan of redemption. Walk with confidence with the banner of apologetics held high.

When we feel a spiritual need, think of Revelation 3:20, offering you the love of God, conversion. Have a convincing proof of apologetics in your mind and on your tongue to stand up against all doubts and satanic forces. Jesus is Lord, must dominate our thoughts with the Beatitudes operational. Be an overcomer. to self, Satan and world. 1st. Peter 5:8, "Be vigilant, be on the alert. Your advisory, the devil, prowls about like a roaring lion, seeking someone to devour." We know we have weak minds as we were born spiritually dead and Satan wants to keep us this way. We can overcome with diligence and a strong apologetic stand. Our motivation is God's love, keep your mind on a spiritual track, do not allow derailment.

With our weak minds of spiritual disinclination, all assurance rests on our strong belief and frequent recall of apologetics, that is, at all times reassurance of God's presence. Our minds are prone to wander and slip into the slop of total self-centeredness, world standards and Satanic influence. Seek hope, joy and peace from his transcendent voice not self, Satan or the world. The God of creation is bound to the gospel by the testimony of Jesus identifying as equal to God. Do I want my endpoint to be self-limited or thoughts that reach eternity?

Qualify the richness of God's love for us to our trust and belief in the gospel, strengthened by apologetics. I want to feel God's love to the maximum. God's love is represented by the sacrifice of Christ on the cross, a once and for all redemption for all past, present and future sins. A total redemption and propitiation for sins. What should be my reasonable response? Do I believe partial or total redemption and forgiveness following Christ's promise from the cross, "It is finished?" Is my God too small? God of all or God at all?

Two possible reasons for our trials. The result of sin activities, or that trials are designed to make us stronger. Both are inadequate, but both hold elements of truth, however are not the complete answer. Trust in Jesus is the only way to eternal life and to experience joy, hope, peace and freedom from guilt. Storms do not impede but encourage trees to have deeper and more secure roots. Adversity and spiritual storms should result in our seeking deeper, stronger spiritual roots, penetrating deep into our core, based upon apologetics. God proves he is the God of love from all the examples of Jesus with the parables. On the question of suffering, Job realized that he knew virtually nothing yet he kept his faith. The same is true with us. The book of Job testifies to the omnipresence of God even when not felt.

If I really believe someone loves me, my thoughts bend totally to that person. I need to remove all the obstacles that attempt to deviate my thoughts of Jesus. Did Christ go to the cross for all your old sins or only a partial number? Was Christ alone adequate for all your sins? What does God want me to understand and do about tragedy? It is not why, but what can I do? The answer is to draw near to him just as Job ultimately realized. Regarding tragedy we simply do not and cannot know why God allows the birth of severely disabled children. Why are some individuals plagued with tragedies for much of their lives while others hardly at all? I don't know. Why is there injustice on every side? I don't know. The questions are endless if we ask why. Instead, we should ask the question, what? What are you saying to me, God what are you doing in my life? What response do you want me to make? This explains the reason the book of Job, thought to be the oldest book in the Bible, 4000 years in age, attempts to explain tragedy, an ageless question. The explanation is that there is no explanation, that we must trust in God's presence and that he has an ultimate plan for each of us. We must believe that God is in control. We have no other choice. God desires that we have a personal relationship with him through Jesus Christ and that is the best answer we have. There are some events of which we have no control. Must have a stayed trust in Jesus. There is no other alternative answer.

Does God allow tragedy to make us focus greater on our need for him? Our time here on earth is short. It is urgent that we clean up our corrupt souls by belief and trust in Jesus at this time and plug into God's love which is on standby. With the seed of belief, implant this into our soul to undergo a progressive metamorphosis, sanctification and to prepare us spiritually for our physical death. The question is not why do bad things happen to us but to understand the urgency of a heartfelt relationship with Jesus, the Holy Spirit. Tragedies may be for that purpose or one of the reasons, thus to motivate us. We are to be urgently aware of our lost status and therefore surrender to Jesus as Lord before our physical death. Tragedy in the world urges us to strongly consider our relationship with God. Jesus as Lord. Self is not important. We must awaken ourselves to the ongoing influence of self, Satan and the world, contributing to the formation of our corrupt thoughts. To overcome, start with apologetic truths.

As Jesus said, "unless you repent, with attitude and thought, you will all likewise perish." Luke 13:3-5. Jesus was far more concerned with a person's eternal well-being than merely satisfying an intellectual curiosity of immediate concerns. Life in this world is frail and uncertain. We cannot boast of tomorrow. It is therefore vital that we correct our neglected relationship with God here and now before physical death and our souls permanently transported to Hades. As in Psalm 90:12, "teach us to realize the brevity of life, that we may grow in wisdom," prayed the psalmist. Repentance and belief are the keys to unlock our brains to understanding the mystery that was previously hidden in the fog of self centeredness. Direct all inner thoughts from selfishness to Beatitude thinking. I trust myself to a resurrected loving God whose control is ultimate and whose wisdom transcends my own feeble understanding. It is too late for submission and conversion after physical death. Die to self, pick up your cross and follow. Repent is the change of our paradigm of thought from self to Beatitude thinking, God first, neighbor second. The God of the cosmos is a God of love and we cannot connect in the absence of a total love and conversion to Jesus as

Lord, as he is the binding connection to our God of the cosmos. John 10:30, "I and the father are one." Our life is hopeless without experiencing God's love.

When you think about God, consider if you were a robot, how your thoughts would be. Confined to a self-limited endpoint, versus our potential with no limit in spiritual thought with trust and belief. There would be no thoughts of God's love, nor the gospel. No fellowship with prayer, supplication, joy, thanksgiving, peace. A robot reading the Bible would read only words, not spiritual joy, peace and hope. Do I act and live as a robot, not allowing the Holy Spirit free reign and control? Robots only respond to preprogrammed reflex actions. Basically not responding to anything beyond a prior mechanical input. This is identical to a lower brainstem reflex response to our sensory receptors with no cerebral cortex input. No hormonal neurotransmitter influence nor to feel subjectively a favorable response to our pondering with rich assurance on God's love. We would not be able to be motivated to reach the expectations to which God sees in us as our potential. God is most happy when we attain our potential, that is, a rich agape fellowship with him. Potential is reached only by encouragement. The reason we have freewill and are not robots is to achieve self-motivation to the excellence that God desires. He desires that we reach our spiritual potential through a living relationship with the Holy Spirit. Proverbs 17:22, "A merry heart is good medicine." Live beyond robotic stature and thought. Wake up, your soul is corrupt and not designed to be limited to the lower brainstem for a limited endpoint. Galatians 5:19, God did not make us a robot. We can therefore overcome suffering by experiencing God's love as the ultimate joy. God's love in our hearts is the antidote to sorrow, fear and superstition. This is only available through a belief in Jesus as Lord. Do not settle for a self-limited spiritual life, as we must plug in with belief and receive God's love, the Holy Spirit.

I do not want to think like a robot and be unaware of God's love. Rather, he desires to move me to spiritual fulfillment. God desires that we enjoy his love and companionship, therefore not a robotic life.

Do I feel like a robot or do I experience God's love? Do I want to have a self-centered life and not experience God's love? Do I want others not to feel my love? The cross, God's love is most important to us. It is important also that we express love to others. When in doubt, focus on the cross, God's love. Concentrate on God's love. He sent Jesus for us to identify with on the cross. Make a habit of telling yourself that God loves you. This life is full of sorrow and self-failure due to self, Satan and world influence. This should draw us to God with the force of a magnet.

My atoms are returned to recycle following physical death. My soul is eternal. To lay treasure in heaven is dependent upon faith in Jesus with a prayer fellowship. Treasures in heaven are dependent upon a strong prayer life. How will we enjoy God in eternity if we are not in this habit now of prayer? Treasures in heaven are strengthened by a relationship, not mantras, idols or attempts to follow good rules or works. Jesus clearly wanted us not to build our hopes and happiness on this life. We live in a fallen evil world, and one day we stand to lose everything except those qualities that have eternal value. He urged us again and again to lay up for yourselves treasures in heaven. Matthew 6:20-21. This is dependent upon us. Treasures in heaven is your prayerful fellowship that reflects the degree of trust we have in Jesus

Christ. We are overcomers only by expressing greater trust. "The steadfast love of the Lord never ceases, His mercies never come to an end, they are new every morning, great is thy faithfulness, the Lord is my portion says my soul, therefore I will hope in him." Lamentations 3:22-24. Humans are different from all forms of life, our spirits live on, our souls, eternal.

First, daily put to death your self-will. As a seed dies, a new life. Metamorphosis is life transformation. God gave us an example through nature, new life through death. Death of the old sin-filled soul, the seed of belief develops with a metamorphosis and transformation in the chrysalis of our souls. Not just a shedding of old skin, the same animal with just a superficial change, but an internal transformation, a new birth. Jesus who created all the cosmos came to end fear, hopelessness, guilt, despair, to give hope and the expectation of eternal life through belief in him as God and our Redeemer. The evidence of apologetics is overwhelming to support Christianity, John 3:17, "for God did not send his Son to the world to condemn the world but that the world would be saved through him." The bottom line of the gospel is the truth of the love of God for each individual. John 3:16, John 10:7-16, the Prodigal son, Revelation 3:20. Ephesians 3:17-19. As a metaphor in nature to illustrate spiritual rebirth, the love of God and our acceptance of Jesus changes the chrysalis of our soul, the conversion of the seed of belief to that of a beautiful spiritual in-flight butterfly with unlimited expectations. New dimensions of life unimaginable to the lonely caterpillar confined in sin, self bondage and limitation. The same feeling is experienced when leaving an alpine hut with morning's first light, the ice cracking beneath our boots on new trails to experience discovery of awaiting magnificent treasures in

God's creation. On many occasions my son and I have been so overwhelmed with a level of exhilaration in panoramic snow and glacier encased mountain peak vistas, stillness on forest paths, alpine orchids dripping with early morning dew, ferns illuminated with rays of light through the trees, we felt we could trek forever without an ultimate destination. An amazing discovery and enjoyable phenomenon to observe that the more delicate alpine flowers will close their petal doors at night, protecting reproductive components from the night cold and promptly without delay open to the first morning warmth of sunlight to display their beautiful petals to attract a variety of eager awaiting pollinators. Some days exceeding 30,000 steps over all surfaces, rock to ice, steep ascents and descents, with backpack, trekking poles, crampons, always present, cautious expectancy and thankfulness.

The reason God chose Jesus to come is to transform fear, guilt, hopelessness to a heavenly hope and confidence by the knowing and assurance of God's enduring, unconditional love for us through the cross and belief. God has promised healing of a guilty conscience, fear and hopelessness. God is infinite. He knows that unconditional love is our greatest desire and need. We are finite in physical, mental and thought capacity. Would you like to have the answer how to replace your insecure and negative thoughts to thoughts of joy and confidence in an omniscient personal Jesus? There is solid evidence of God in Christ through apologetics, general and specific revelation.

1. Creation and the cosmos is evidence of God's presence, even at this moment in time.

2. Our conscience is evidence of Gods implanted behavioral parameters in our minds and our need for God due to internal conflicts with these parameters.

3. The claims of Jesus and the historical evidence of the validity of the gospel binds evidence of God to Jesus. Jesus claimed to be equal to God on many occasions, thus identifying him to the God of the cosmos.

4. God's word written over a period of 1500 years by 40 different authors. The golden thread to express the common denominator of hope for mankind through faith in God and a saving Redeemer gives continuity to all the authors.

Our limited finite outlook on this life can be transformed with the belief in the resurrection of Christ and eternal life with God. Psalm 16. Why is it difficult to believe in God's love for you. He went to the cross while we were still embedded in sin and he chose to demonstrate his unselfish love for us, on the cross. This should be my last thought of the night and my first thought in the morning. This should determine my mental profile for the entire day. Thanking God daily for grace, mercy and forgiveness and with every view of creation as an apologetic reminder of his graciousness.

God removed the scales of unbelief from our eyes following our belief in the historical Jesus. Our knowledge of God's love for us must be heartfelt. This results in a strong affirmative prayer life. This consistency in prayer is designed to lay up treasures in heaven. The belief of Jesus as Lord will remove the scales by grace from our eyes of spiritual disinclination. We have no other avenue to eternity but to thank Jesus for his unfailing love, from the epiphany and gift from apologetic belief in the total gospel of Jesus. Reinforced with a strong prayer life, his unfailing love, the cross and the presence of the Holy Spirit.

How do we know his unfailing love? Dependent upon our belief in general and specific apologetic revelation and God's gift to us of belief in Jesus Christ. Creation, conscience, gospel, God's word, all designed to give hope. If you believe apologetics then you are compelled to believe Jesus as Lord as this was his claim on multiple occasions. My apologetics must be accompanied with a Jesus as Lord trust. We do not always feel it but we have the assurance that he is always present, the promised Holy Spirit. We will not change if we do not address the eternal significance of the corruption of our soul which contains the history and totality of our self-centeredness, Satan and world influence of our words, behavior and character. The number one Beatitude, blessed are the poor in spirit. If addressed with honesty, transparency and humility, we must recognize the corruption of our soul. We must change the way we approach our thought life, with Beatitude thinking. If we did not have a conscience, we would be a robot with no feelings, just responsive to our sensory receptors with lower brainstem reflexes and no thought of life after death. Why do we shortchange ourselves and live in the confines of a sealed box? Do I live like a robot dominated by the lower brainstem or am I strong in the Beatitudes to mold my thoughts with Jesus as Lord determining my beliefs and actions?

"UNIVERSAL QUESTION
OF ALL MEN...
WHERE IS GOD?"

"FIVE BILLION OF OUR BROTHERS AND SISTERS ARE IN BONDAGE LOOKING IN THE WRONG DIRECTION"

136

Yes, the atoms in my body are recycled but my spirit and soul is eternal. Therefore, I must nourish a Spirit filled thought life, based upon and consistent, with Jesus as Lord. Our conscience makes us aware of a corrupt, poor-in-spirit soul. This should motivate us as we understand the final destination of a corrupt soul, Hades. God gave us a conscience to help us stay on a healthy mental and physical path, that is, to enjoy God's love without a self imposed impedance. When we deviate, we feel guilt as a function of our conscience. When guilt dominates our mental chambers, it impedes our receiving and acceptance of God's love as we feel undeserving. God knows mankind's weakness and our proclivity of sensitivity to guilt, self degradation and feelings of unworthiness. Prior cultures and some today responding to this issue attempt and attempted to solve with multiple gods, icons and satanic inspired sacrifices.

As God made us, he provided a solution. Belief in Jesus and the cross; "It is finished", thus we are justified by faith (an ongoing belief) reflected by evidence of the presence of the fruit of the spirit. Love, joy, peace, patience, kindness, goodness, faithfulness, gentleness and self-control. Is my soul redeemed? Am I grafted to the Holy Spirit? Free from bondage to mental impedance and self degradation, now receptive to God's love and thoughts of eternal glory? We must focus daily on God's unconditional love. Joy is the external expression of inward spiritual confidence, that is, enjoying this cognitive confidence and the physiological and psychological benefits of elevated neurohormones, dopamine, serotonin and oxytocin acting upon their respective neurons and neural synapses.

Praise God for these medical revelations that reveal God's plan through awareness of his fellowship to maximize our health. When we know the love of God, the cross, deep in our heart for ourselves and believe in life after death or life through death to self, our outlook on this life with all its pains and sorrows will be transformed, with the peace of God experienced now.

A peace that transcends all human understanding, an epiphany that Paul experienced, filled and sustained him for 30 years until his martyrdom. Never lose sight that belief opens the door of God's love, the Holy Spirit, a socket-and-plug relationship, Revelation 3:20. The only love permanent and unconditional. God put you and me here to have a love relationship with him. Are you truly spiritually alive or still struggling with the burden of sin and self, carrying the tightly bound rotting corpse of sin, unbelief and spiritual death? Paul traveled his 13,000 miles for 30 years preaching the answer. Romans 8:1-2,"There is now no condemnation for those who are in Christ Jesus. For the of the law of the Spirit of life in Christ Jesus has set you free from the law of sin and of death."

The Old Testament religion had turned faith in God into rules that could not be kept, resulting with chronic guilt and secularization to a work-based religion and commercialization of religious practice, the sacrificial system and self-styled rabbinical control. Similar to that experienced today of any religious system that does not focus on Jesus, but seeks monetary gains at the expense by controlling the members through guilt and obedience to tradition over belief in the saving grace of Jesus. Corrupt money changers filled the temple area and secular laws governed the religious ceremonial holidays. Jesus came to lead people to a correct relationship with God, repentance, belief, surrender to his lordship and a one-on-one prayer fellowship, with the cross and resurrection as evidence of his divinity. The focus and acceptance of

God's love is the foundation of hope, joy and peace. Romans 15:13. This requires surrender of self, to trust in Jesus as Lord and belief in the gospel. Fears and superstitions dominated the daily life when Jesus arrived. Let's do away with all fears. We must believe something, logic and reason point to Christ. Jesus points us in the direction of belief followed by faith, with an ongoing walk by faith, not by sight or feelings.

Fear and guilt have been described as our greatest threat to mental health as so universally ubiquitous. It robs our minds of peace. This distorts our understanding, magnifies our problems, ruins our health and promotes abnormal behavior, paralyzing our thinking, trusting and loving. The cure is the discovery of belief in Christ through apologetics followed by repentance and total surrender to Jesus as Lord. How to eliminate fear and guilt? Believe and acknowledge God's presence, facilitated by apologetics. Communicate with prayer and be submerged in his love for you as illustrated and demonstrated by the cross. Oppressive fear and guilt is an impediment to professing belief and leads to physical and mental negative manifestations, contrasted to faith. Romans 15:13.

Over 50% of all doctor visits are solely for the determination of reassurance, a significant number of these visits are for unresolved spiritual related issues. This is an important factor to consider when designing a universal health plan that would fail to encourage personal responsibility. This would result in over-utilization with inevitable failure to be cost-effective. We must address personal responsibility in designing the program, and include incentives, for example, tax benefits to encourage and motivate people to pursue healthy habits of behavior including diet and physical exercise. In addition, mandatory sliding scale payments dependent upon income should be required for all outpatient visits. I have concluded from observing various European single-payer health systems that self-esteem and personal responsibility play a key role in success as the stronger the spiritual component of a population group, the stronger the mental health, thus less abuse and unnecessary utilization of the health system. Further evidence to encourage the constant healthy presence of our hormonal neurotransmitters, facilitated by the enjoyment of God's love.

We must eliminate doubts and fears with 100% trust in God's love, the cross, Revelation 3:20, the Prodigal Son, John 3:16, Ephesians 3:17-19. Jesus stands at the door, rings a bell with the offer to come in and fellowship. Rather than fixed on negative issues, know and feel God's love in your inner being, with hope, joy, peace and the promise of eternal life. Fear promotes an elevated cortisol baseline blood level leading to stress resulting in damage from long term exposure to your most vulnerable vital organs whose function may have been marginalized from either a genetic predisposition defect, a chronic disease trajectory, prior trauma or toxic substance abuse. "Thou will keep him in perfect peace whose mind is stayed on thee," Isaiah 26:3.

We may not feel the presence of God but he is there. We don't understand trials but we can trust and believe in his love for us and his presence. Romans 8:28-39. Trust in his presence and unconditional love for you. I want my thoughts to germinate with the Beatitudes, for my words, actions, habits and character. Not to be obsessed with self, but Jesus as Lord as my focus. Take up and carry your cross daily of death to self. We must experience a metamorphosis of our souls now before we die, with the Holy Spirit in command. Not self, not the world, not Satan. Psalm 118:24, "This is the day the Lord has made, let us rejoice and be glad in it." Keep eternity at the apex of our thinking. Be an overcomer to self, Satan and the world. Die to self, with the seed of belief implanted in our soul for conversion and a change in our lives and character. To carry our cross is an ongoing command to die to our corrupt soul, as Jesus carried the sin of the world to Golgotha, Calvary. Every morning consider the question, what does God have planned for me to enjoy today? Look for it. This is the antithesis of chronic daily fear, be thankful. Live one day at a time and enjoy each day as a gift from God. Again,"this is the day the Lord has made, let us rejoice and be glad in it." Psalm 118:24. We need to appreciate life on a moment by moment interval. We have no idea of the totality of events for tomorrow. Continually thank God for the truth of his Word and the work of the Spirit within me.

Find and memorize scripture of God's love for Homo sapiens, Romans 8:28-39. When we look only to self, the end result is self-limited, an all negative final endpoint, self-implosion, hopelessness versus Jesus as Lord with an endpoint of eternal joy. With all other life creations, the physical body of atoms are recycled, no spiritual component. We were provided as humans such a remarkable spiritual capacity that sadly has either been perverted by Satan or remains dormant due to self-preoccupation or an overriding disinclination to our God given thoughts of eternity. One day we all stand to lose everything in this world, and no one knows when that day will arrive. Once we have given our lives to God, we belong eternally to him, and in Christ we have all that is ultimately important. If we spend our time worrying about ourselves, we have missed the whole point of our existence. Look to yourself and in the long run you will find hatred, loneliness, despair, rage, ruin, foolishness, vanity and decay. Our natural endpoint does not go beyond self-imposed desperations. We understand and believe God's unconditional love for us as told and retold throughout the Bible, direct and in parables. We must have a metamorphosis from the seed of belief before physical death, otherwise it is too late. If we experience a metamorphosis, then our souls become flushed clean, dominated by our faith, Jesus as Lord. Apologetics promote belief, faith and regeneration of our souls.

He stands at everyone's door and knocks. There is no security in self as an endpoint. When we open the door of belief to God's love, Christ enters, Jesus as Lord. This is the only source of love and security that ultimately makes sense. God is with us, omnipresent. After death, we live in a relationship with Jesus. It is therefore important to experience now at this time an intimate relationship with my Helper, Paraclete, that Jesus said he would send us to those who believe. Sin, pride, self-rule impede this relationship. We must totally surrender to his Lordship now and the seed to our soul for conversion. This belief process is facilitated by the apologetics of general revelation; creation and conscience. Specific revelation; historic gospel, resurrection, God's word. We do not consider our inevitable death until we see it on the horizon as I did one year ago. That view of oncoming death motivates us to consider the corruption of our eternal soul. There is no second chance if we continue in a state of spiritual death prior to physical death. There are three deaths for us. We are born spiritually dead.

God offers us a cure with His love and a new spiritual birth, dependent upon our belief in the gospel with faith following. Spiritual death is our natural state at birth, progressively filled with self-limitations, fears, anger, hopelessness, guilt, a corrupt conscience, completely self centered, me first. If we die in a state of spiritual death which is all thought devoid of our true creator, our body disintegrates with atoms returning to the physical world to recycle, our soul released to the abyss of Hades. This is a one way street, there is no return. This is why it is so important that belief and a metamorphosis of our soul occurs prior to physical death. Luke 16:19-31. There is only one road to Heaven. John 14:6, "I am the way, the truth, the life, no one goes to the father except by me."

A second death is that of physical death. If physical death occurs prior to the initiation of regeneration, that of conversion of our soul, all is lost. No second chance. Our final judgment decree has been written. Eternal death is a result of final judgment, a result of self-rule, absent faith in Jesus, a corrupt soul reflecting negative character traits, Galatians 5:19. A corrupt dead soul is a character filled with fear, guilt and hopelessness as the end-point. Again this must be addressed while we are still alive at the time of recognizing our spiritually dead corrupt soul status. Start with a serious study of apologetics, general and specific. God's gift is the recognition of Jesus Christ as the answer to our dead condition, decaying corrupt soul. Eternal death results in our permanent location to Hades, in the abyss, lake of fire. There is no opportunity for redemption.

Consider the resemblance between a small seed sown in the ground, the seed of belief to our soul, and the result of a lovely flower developing from it, our spiritual sanctification. The new birth cannot be imagined prior to this metamorphosis resulting in a new spiritual body. 1st. Corinthians 2:9-10. To be right with God we must experience conversion now at this time before it is too late. Luke 16:19-31. God gives us multiple examples in nature of the results of metamorphosis, a new birth. If he can do this with physical life forms, he can do this with us in the spiritual realm. We should recognize his desire that we understand these examples in nature as applied to our spiritual potential. It was God's humor that he gave us these lower forms of metamorphosis in nature to expose a potential that we can reach spiritually. A complete change from inside out. No recognition of the prior being. A marvel of transformation. Though God desires that we choose to come, he does not need us, we need him, considering the importance of final judgment of a corrupt soul. If we are not rooted and grounded in the love of God, the cross, we cannot escape his righteous judgment. If we rule God out of our lives, we are ruled out of his, if we refuse to open the door and do not want his forgiveness, we shall not have it. Realize the nails of the cross piercing the hands and feet of Jesus our Redeemer. Visualize the torn temple veil. Also visualize the result and magnificence of examples of metamorphosis, rebirth, the butterfly and the frog and our spiritual metamorphosis and endpoint with Jesus. Reassuring to the polliwog is a species specific guarantee of one to seven months for completion of metamorphosis. Of equal reassurance to us is Philippians 1:6, "And so I am sure that God who began this good work in you will carry it on until it is finished on the day of Christ Jesus." Metamorphosis in the physical world is remarkably complex for us to visualize or understand the how and why. The same with spiritual metamorphosis. The results of a physical metamorphosis in the animal kingdom is always an improvement. The same result with a spiritual metamorphosis, a door to eternity opens, an exit from the evils and tribulations of this world. 1st. Peter 1:23-24, "for you have been born again not of seed which is perishable but imperishable, that is, through the living and abiding word of God. For, All flesh is like grass, and all its glory like the flower of grass. The grass withers, and the flower falls off, but the word of the Lord abides forever." We cannot understand or explain, just have to observe and experience it. We must realize that the metamorphosis in the plant and pre-human animal kingdom is temporal and that a spiritual metamorphosis for us is eternal in dimension and promise.

A child believes the ultimate joy and pleasure in life to be various sweets and treats. An adult believes the ultimate joy and pleasure to experience is sexual encounter and ego. The joys and pleasures to be experienced in heaven are beyond all imagination. God created all pleasures and in no way will earthly pleasures compare to eternal pleasures. "Blessed be the God and father of our Lord Jesus Christ. By his great mercy we have been born to a new living hope through the resurrection of Jesus Christ from the dead, and to an inheritance which is imperishable, undefiled and unfading, kept in heaven for you." 1st Peter 1:3. Peter knew all this to be true, not just theory, risking his life and limb on this verse he wrote. The greatest deterrent to avoid sin is my heart filled with the expectation of heaven's glory. Short scuffles with temptation and trials "are not worthy to be compared with the glory which shall be revealed to us," Romans 8:18. Not too distant in the future.

Everything is dependent upon what we do after realizing the condition of our souls in our natural state of spiritual death and corruption and our long-standing history of a spiritual disinclination. We decide either self or a new seed, Jesus is Lord, implanted, followed by a metamorphosis and sanctification, a conversion of our souls. God's love is laid in our hearts only following the opening of the door of belief to the awaiting love of Jesus. Revelation 3:20. Belief is a gift of God following our apologetic enlightenment of the truth of the

145

historical Jesus. Do I live the Beatitudes? Do I feel the love of Jesus and omnipresence of the Holy Spirit as my most intimate friend? We must practice by habit the Beatitudes as evidence for a Jesus-led implantation of new thinking and behavior, only possible with the help of the Holy Spirit.

The annals of history have proven that those who have contributed most to social justice are those who have lived with Christ at the forefront of their minds. The secret to making a difference in the world is to believe that God works through you; to live the Beatitudes, to incorporate and pursue the best of your proclivities, inner desires and talents, rewarded as a result of service to man. Truly, we reap what we sow. 2nd. Corinthians 5:9-20, Galatians 6:7-9, Job 4:8-9, 2nd. Corinthians 9:6. A fascinating, motivational, enjoyable, resource pertaining to this subject, Rusten, E. Michael and Sharon. "The One Year Book of Christian History." Tyndale House, 2003. Live daily with the expectation of Christ's return. Are you ready to meet the Lord?

From the teachings of Jesus, it seems that at the moment of death there will be a great divide between those who know and love God, and those who do not. An amazing number of parables indicate this division. The Wheat and the Tares, the Sheep and the Goats, the Great Banquet, the Rich Fool, the Wise and Foolish Bridesmaids, those with or without wedding garments, The Dragnet of Good and Bad Fish, the House on the Rock and a House in the Sand. The message of Jesus is not only the proclamation of salvation but the announcement of judgment, a cry of warning and a call to repentance in view of the terrible urgency of the crisis. Repentance is to change from self to total surrender to Jesus as Lord and to begin Beatitude thinking determining our behavior. Judgment is on the horizon. Everything depends upon total surrender of our souls to Jesus as Lord and God's love, dependent upon our belief in Jesus as Lord in our hearts. This must be accomplished while we are still alive, for after our souls leave our body at physical death, it is too late. Final judgment for our souls will be either the lake of fire or eternity with God. This is our most important decision in this life. What is your most important date? The day of judgment is my most important date. When I fall asleep at night, am I ready to meet Jesus? Thank God every day for grace, mercy, forgiveness, peace, joy, hope and the expectation to be with him. The validity of the historical Jesus is indisputable. Have I responded as so many parables illustrate? These are important metaphors to Jesus' message on how to motivate a person out of spiritual death, to be born again, a conversion. A new life in identification with Jesus as Lord and our surrender of self. Do I celebrate with prayer and fellowship now?

"We know that when Christ appears, we shall be like him, because we shall see him as he really is." 1st John 3:2. A transformation of our bodies into the likeness of Him. Heaven is being with Christ. The Christian is not preparing for death, he is preparing for life. Abundant life in all its fullness. The world with it's fleeting pleasures is not the final reality. Eternal life begins as soon as we receive Christ as our Savior. We can start enjoying it now for a quality of life beyond our imagination. 1st Corinthians 2:9-10. Free of guilt, fear, hopelessness and the promise of eternal life. The result of the crucifixion, redemption for those who believe in the Lordship of Christ, tearing of the temple veil allowing access to God's presence, love and forgiveness through trust in Jesus Christ. Be diligent and believe. "Even though I walk through the valley of the shadow of death I will fear no evil for Thou art with me." Psalm 23:4. Be ready to identify with the complete gospel to explain your faith, hope, and with apologetics, the evidence of God's presence in creation, conscience, the gospel of Jesus and God's word. 1st Peter 3:15, "Sanctify Christ as Lord in your heart, always be ready to make a defense to everyone who asks you to give an account for the hope that is in you, yet with gentleness and reverence." Enjoy and relish moment by moment God's love for you.

Thanksgiving throughout the day displaces worry and anxiety. Awaken each day with thanksgiving. Cultivate awareness of the omnipresence of God, the Holy Spirit and His constant love for you. Mother Teresa said to her dentist, a friend of mine, "in eternity, all bad earthly experiences will seem like one night spent in a bad hotel room." Keeping the joy of heaven always before you will help you to run your race with patience. Jesus came to dispel fear, superstition, hopelessness, guilt, and anxiety. The cross and resurrection are the pivot points of belief. God's love is the result of accepting God's knock on the door of your heart and accepting his invitation for fellowship, the permanent grafting into an indwelling Holy Spirit, following belief in Jesus Christ. This is urgent, do I follow the new paradigm, transformation and conversion leading to dominant Beatitude thinking or am I stuck in the idol of self and spiritual death as a result of an aborted seed or a stillbirth in the soul? We now can live with hope, joy, and peace. Romans 15:13. Be an overcomer and be transformed by the renewing of your mind and thoughts. Romans 12:1-2. Repent and renew your thinking with the Beatitudes.

The total panorama of our lives can be explained as we were born to spiritual death, self rule, and self-limited sensual goals that do not satisfy. Fear, anguish, guilt, hopelessness and false idols, superstition, no satisfaction. We seek temporal substitutes to satisfy.

Greed, sex and overindulgence, yet nothing satisfies our void in the presence of compensatory and increasing sensual appetites. One must understand that the current and future consequences of our corrupt soul is eternal death. The door to open our void is God's love dependent upon belief in the gospel which is a gift from God based upon our apologetic epiphany of the historical Christ. Surrender to the metamorphosis from the seed of belief, Jesus as Lord. There is no other way. There is only one gate, one path, and only one Shepherd who loves you, to solve our corrupt soul healing. The goal is to change our soul from corrupt to contagious. We must void and replace self-rule, repent, and carry our cross daily.

The bottom line of the Beatitudes is God first and neighbor second, characterized by diligence, honesty and transparency. Be sympathetic, authentic to others, respect but not condescending. Control and monitor all thoughts to the obedience of Christ. 2nd. Corinthians 10:5. Explain the reason for the hope you have in you, keep apologetics on the edge of your tongue. If there is no love relationship with the Holy Spirit, our well-being for now and eternity, is total failure. All is dependent on a heartfelt belief in the gospel and my priority to see Jesus as Lord. Don't just say it, live it. Ephesians 4:22-24, Ezekiel 36:24-27. Mere mental assent and agreement to these truths will not liberate us as long as we are in bondage to self as god. Must live a life of total surrender of all cerebral compartments to the Lordship of Christ. Our freedom must be seen in our daily lives. Freedom from sin's bondage is evidenced by living totally in the embrace of Jesus, motivated by his love.

There are two kinds of Christians. Those driven by fear and uncertainty on the one hand and those driven by expectation and joy on the other. The former are locked into partial belief in the cross and poisoned by a vacillating surrender to Jesus. Our only hope is maximizing our pleasures in God by a total and complete surrender to Jesus as Lord. The Christian walk is not about trying harder but enjoying freedom from bondage to self, by the restoration of a corrupt, guilt and sin filled soul, through a new birth of progressive sanctification. A transformation of the seed of belief and living in the presence of the Holy Spirit.

How did Paul replace troubling thoughts arising from the subconscious as reported in Chapter 7 of Romans and arrive to the riches of a life in Chapter 8? In Chapter 7, Paul describes a common struggle of Christians on the spiritual path, prior to a total surrender and commitment to the Lordship of Christ of all compartments of their conscious being. This struggle with the lower brainstem, sensory and response complex of Chapter 7 reflects a dominance of the subconscious determining our thought expression, resulting in an individual feeling hypocritical and unworthy of God's love, a failure, Satan's delight.

151

KINDNESS AND
ENCOURAGEMENT
ARE CONTAGIOUS

153

It is obvious and morbidly satisfying that for a period of time even Paul experienced this difficult struggle as we have, and do, between the lower brainstem reflexes, the subconscious, belief in total forgiveness and impedance to allow the Holy Spirit total access and influence to all cerebral storage compartments. Christ will not occupy an evil filled chamber, only if sin free, no hypocrisy. Guilt thus absent if Christ present. It is also possible that Paul was describing this common human impediment for total commitment and our recurrent proclivity as humans to intermittently lay aside our cross, thus allowing the old nature to dominate. To the question by Paul in Romans 7:24, "who will free me from this body of sin and death?" It is unclear if Paul was referencing mythology or claims of an ancient Roman practice that a convicted murderer had the corpse of his victim bound to his body, face to face, shoulder to shoulder, mouth to mouth, hand to hand. This rotting corpse a constant reminder of his guilt and conviction. Under penalty of death no one was allowed to remove the body.

This describes our life prior to belief and complete surrender of self to the cross of Jesus who then took away our tightly bound rotting corpse of sin, past, present and future. A new self image of freedom, no longer in bondage to this self image of conviction and defeat, but now to rest in the arms of Jesus, to lie down in green pastures, led by still waters, the restoration of my soul, to walk in the ways of righteousness of God first and neighbor second; the Beatitudes. No longer in bondage commanded and governed by the lower brainstem and a perverted corrupt soul. Freedom from a life attached to rotting flesh, self first, instead replaced with the resurrected Jesus as my Lord and Shepherd. Christ's redemption removed the rotting corpse of death, sin and failure that was tightly bound to my body which dominated my being prior to a heartfelt belief, rebirth, sanctification and indwelling Holy Spirit Paraclete. I must walk the walk. Hebrews 12:14, "...without holiness no one will see the Lord."

This process of redemption was a fulfillment of his eternal plan to rescue us through his torture and dying in our place, surgically extirpating our corpse of sin with his demise on the cross.

Isaiah 53:5	John 3;17
Romans 12:1-3	Isaiah 40:31
2nd. Corinthians 5:17	Romans 6:11
Ephesians 4:22-24	Philippians 3:13-14

Our submission to and the indwelling of the Holy Spirit as discussed in chapter 8 is evidence of our heartfelt belief and **total surrender** that results in behavioral change. Not just our head knowledge. This is the "truth that has set us free." John 8:32. "For all have sin and fall short of the glory of God," Romans 3:23. "God sent his son into the world not to judge the world but to save the world through Him," John 3:17. Jesus desires that we enjoy this life to its fullest and in Matthew 7:7-8 states, "Ask, and it shall be given you; seek, and ye shall find; knock, and it shall be opened unto you; for everyone that asketh receiveth; and he that seeketh findeth; and to him that knocketh it shall be opened."

Only when we acknowledge that we are totally emancipated from the bondage of the rotting corpse of sin, self, are we able to attain the chief end of man. "To glorify God and enjoy Him forever." We must remind ourselves of total redemption, "it is finished." We glorify God through spiritual growth. Our cerebral cortex must always be in the capacity of **dominant** engagement to purify neurologic responses. Remember to apply the five second delayed response rule, so if a negative thought; as a hot cinder falls on you, immediately extinguish the invading rubbish and follow with God's beautiful filter of Philippians 4:8, whatever is **TRUE, NOBLE, JUST, PURE, LOVELY, GOOD REPORT, VIRTUE, WORTHY OF PRAISE**. Only with hesitation, diligence, repetition and application will we establish these new habits of thought in forming responses. So important. Easy to say, difficult to overcome old habits. "For as he thinketh in his heart, so is he." Proverbs 23:7.

Jesus has gifted believers the Holy Spirit to help overcome this conflict of our sin nature, expressed through the lower brainstem. Without his indwelling presence we have no hope of conquering our old habits. To overcome requires our **total** and **complete** surrender of all chambers of our being. The drainage pipe must be clean. The lower brainstem is a permanent neurological component of all animals, designed for rapid fight and flight response with little or no cerebral input. As the surprised gazelle responds to a charging lion. In addition to this function in humans for survival designed fight and flight, most sin proclivities are expressed through the same neurological pathways. The Holy Spirit, allowed free access to all our mental compartments can overcome embedded neural pathways of sin with replacement of a stronger conscious presence of a reward of love and the promise of eternal life, before they are compounded into aberrant undesirable responses. Our diligence to obey the Holy Spirit and desire to flush the corrupt soul will result in our overcoming this proclivity to a sensory and reflex response. The replacement functional pivot is the promise of God's abundant love, joy and the expectation of spending eternity with Him. John 14:2-6. Paul describes the solution for the replacement of self, a proven failure dominated by the lower brainstem, with a stronger power, the Holy Spirit, indwelling as my Paraclete following total surrender to his Lordship. Chapter 8 of Romans would be wise for us to memorize for recall and confidence building.

The God of the cosmos provided this confidence for all believers through the sacrificial cross of Christ, the tearing open of the veil, redemption, justification, sanctification, the indwelling Holy Spirit, his promise of sonship for us and promise of eternal life. "For I am convinced that neither death nor life, neither angels nor demons, neither the present nor the future nor any powers, neither height nor depth, nor anything else in all creation will be able to separate us from the love of God that is in Christ Jesus our Lord." Romans 8:38-39. This explains Paul's passion, fueled by grace, that he had no apparent residual guilt.

Paul's greatest motivation was his joy of God's love for him, belief in righteousness by faith alone, the resurrection of Jesus Christ, his love of ambassadorship and the anticipation of his crown of righteousness reward. In A.D. 61, during his first imprisonment in Rome, Paul wrote in Ephesians 6:19-20, "and pray on my behalf, that utterance may be given to me in the opening of my mouth, to make known with boldness the mystery of the gospel, for which I am an ambassador in chains; that in proclaiming it I may speak boldly, as I ought to speak." Even in prison Paul was not thinking of his own welfare but of his testimony for Christ.

Tychicus carried this letter to Ephesus with the greeting of grace and peace written in the beginning and again at the end of the letter. As mentioned earlier, should we not be in the habit to express this same greeting for sincere encouragement to reach those who have a hidden need?

With Christ's death and the tearing of the temple veil representing man's sin barrier to the Holy of Holies, God, we now can confidently rest in his love and live a life as an overcomer with the Holy Spirit indwelling as our loving Paraclete. In efforts to seek righteous behavior, replacement therapy has long been successfully employed in psychiatry, secular and religious cultures. Ulysses, the ancient mariner, overcame temptation of the music of the Sirens, the demonic cannibals who would lure their victims with irresistible song to the shallow reefs of their island with destruction of the mariners' vessel. Ulysses overcame this sensual temptation only by latching himself to the mast and demanding the sailors to tightly fix wax in their ears. Temptation was overcome only by struggle and fighting the sensory pleasing urge of the music. Jason, also a character of ancient mythology, solved the temptation ending with destruction by taking along on his journey Orpheus, an extremely talented musician who filled the air with a far greater melodious sound that had greater captivation to both crew and captain. Safe passage filled with song and joy overcame the temptation from the Sirens. Temptation was replaced by a more pleasing reward.

BEAUTIFUL PEOPLE
MADE IN GOD'S IMAGE
WITH SOUL AND SPIRIT

Paul's dominant replacement thoughts were the cherished joys of being an ambassador for Christ, the expectation of the reward of the crown of righteousness and the surety to be in the eternal presence of God. If the God of the cosmos designed all life; and humans with spirit and soul, then in his genius he provided a way for us to reject unhealthy temptations and sin to soul and body that would hold us in captivity, bondage, hopelessness, fear, guilt, and to self-disparagement. 1st. Corinthians 10:13, Galatians 5:16-25. He gave us the ability to appreciate and recognize a greater reward to our souls in order to overcome temptations. As the greater power and thrust of aerodynamics overcomes gravitational force. Yes, the music of the Sirens has an overwhelming appeal to temptation, yet the heartfelt belief in Jesus gives us a replacement of greater joy with personal fellowship, eternal expectations following death and a richness added to our soul. One must not forget that in enjoying God's love our hormonal neurotransmitters are elevated which improves our health status, resulting from our choice to focus on His precious love.

My daily walk should not be a struggle to suppress desires from self, Satan or world standards, but to listen to His transcendent voice which will yield far greater pleasure and rewards from righteous thoughts and behavior. Thank daily the Creator of the cosmos for all he desires that I recognize of his joys for me to experience this day. His works and plans for me will thus be revealed if I look at each day from his perspective. Be open to look for them rather than a negative and critical view of life and people. One of my joys is to daily look away from the challenge of the day and up to a beautiful blue sky when present, with puffy white cloud clusters gracefully changing in design every moment and think of them as footprints of Christ, a reminder of his omnipresence and the beauty of his creation.

How do we strengthen our current level of faith?

1. Always meditate to include rumination, for stronger ingrained neural pathways. A must to include scripture, pertaining to total forgiveness, and our acceptance through Christ's sacrifice.

2. Study with the same diligence scripture pertaining to the promise of Christ's life in you. "The hope of glory." Colossians 1:27.

3. Arm yourself with memorization and rumination on the word of God to fix firmly new neural pathways for righteousness in thought and behavior with the intent and desire to prevail over the subconscious and unconscious brain.

4. Strengthen the habit of scripture recall when receiving a sin-filled Trojan Horse delivered to the cerebral cortex from either internal or external sources.

5. Make no provision for the flesh receptors of the lower brainstem to dominate our response mechanisms. Rather, as a result of our total surrender to the Lordship of Christ, integrate and apply replacement therapy, via our newly strengthened neural pathways and synapses of the cerebral cortex to respond with appropriate righteous thoughts and behavior.

We may assume that the final instructions from Jesus to his eleven disciples dictated his most highly valued thoughts and concerns. Matthew 28:19-20 "Go therefore and make disciples of all nations, baptizing them in the name of the Father and the Son and the Holy Spirit, teaching them to observe all that I commanded you; and lo I am with you always, even to the end of the age." These words of Jesus emphasize his desire for a universal individual spiritual rebirth of every man's corrupt soul, a total surrender to the Lordship of Christ and to live his precepts. Notably the last instruction from the God of the cosmos was his desire for individual spiritual rebirth with no mention of the inclusion of the goals for material comforts, social status or objectives for personal gain. Where therefore should our focus, thoughts, desires and goals, be directed during these last days? In your last moments, do you desire your nostrils filled with the stench of death, decay and loss or the welcoming fragrance of an eternal spring?

Finally, we rest on these promises, a new spiritual body and a new spiritual alpine inn beyond our fondest imagination including eternal panoramas beyond imagination. 2nd. Corinthians 5:1, "For we know that if the earthly tent which is our house is torn down, we have a building from God, a house he himself has made, which will last forever." John 14:1-3,"let not your heart be troubled; believe in God, believe also in me. In my Father's house are many dwelling places; if it were not so, I would have told you; for I go to prepare a place for you. And if I go and prepare a place for you, I will come again and receive you to myself; that where I am, you may be there also." John 11:25-27, "Jesus said to her, I am the resurrection and the life. Those who believe in me will live, even though they die; and all those who live and believe in me will never die.

Do you believe this?" "Yes, Lord!" she answered. "I do believe that you are the Messiah, the Son of God, who was to come into the world."

Enjoy and practice the presence of the Holy Spirit through a total surrender to Jesus Christ as Lord. As the ocean tide flushes twice a day the inner estuaries, so allow an equal process to undesirable cerebral contamination. Hebrews 12:14, "...without holiness you will not see God." Do you have ears to hear the knocking?

I hope this book pierces an opening in your soul membrane, exposing the contents as they seep out. Please let me know if I can be of any help.

In God's love,

Ralph Kemp

seabrightralph@gmail.com

THERE IS NO DEATH

John Luckey McCreery

There is no death! the stars go down

To rise upon some other shore,

And bright in heaven's jeweled crown

They shine for evermore.

There is no death! the forest leaves

 Convert to life the wireless air;

 The rocks disorganized to feed

The hungry moss they bear.

There is no death! the dust we tread

Shall change, beneath the summer showers.

To golden grain, or mellow fruit,

Or rainbow-tinted flowers.

There is no death! the leaves may fall,

The flowers may fade and pass away--

They only wait, through wintry hours,

The warm, sweet breath of May.

There is no death! the choicest gifts

That heaven hath kindly lent to earth

Are ever first to seek again

The country of their birth;

And all things that for growth or joy

Are worthy of our love or care,

Whose loss has left us desolate,

Are safely garnered there.

Though life become a desert waste,

We know it's fairest sweetest flowers,

Transplanted into paradise,

Adorn immortal bowers.

The voice of birdlike melody

That we have missed and mourned so long

Now mingles with the angel choir

In everlasting song.

There is no death! although we grieve

When beautiful, familiar forms

That we have learned to love are torn

From our embracing arms,

Although with bowed and breaking heart,

With sable garb and silent tread,

We bear their senseless dust to rest,

And say that they are "dead,"--

They are not dead! they have but passed

Beyond the mists that blind us here,

Into the new and larger life

Or that serener sphere.

They have but dropped their robe of clay

To put their shining raiment on;

They have not wandered far away,--

They are not "lost," nor "gone."

Though disenthralled and glorified,

They still are here and love us yet;

The dear ones they have left behind

They never can forget.

And sometimes,

When our hearts grow faint

Amid temptations fierce and deep,

Or when the wildly raging waves

Of grief or passion sweep,

We feel upon our fevered brow

Their gentle touch, their breath of balm,

Their arms enfold us, and our hearts

Grow comforted and calm.

And ever near us, though unseen,

The dear, immortal spirits tread--

For all the boundless universe

Is Life:-- there are no dead!

— Written in 1883 by John Luckey McCreery, who was the son of a Methodist minister. He died age 70 from complications of an appendectomy, 1906.

O death, where is thy sting? O grave, where is thy victory?

But thanks be to God, which giveth us victory through our Lord Jesus Christ. 1st. Corinthians 15:55,57.

A FAVORITE RESPITE
BENCH BENEATH
THE TREE AT THIS
CURVE OF "WEG DER
SCHWEIZ" TRAIL,
SOUTH OF SEELISBERG
ON THE CLIFFS OVER
VIERWALDSTATTERSEE.

amazon books

MOD

Order Number: **238956494**

Ordered On: **9/26/2018 11:18:01 AM**

Item ID: **AMZ-B106584**

Cover ID:

Book Block ID:

AMZ-C106584

AMZ-B106584

The Lord Is My Shepherd

*The How and Why to Become Right
With God Before One's Last Breath*

The Lord Is My Shepherd

by Ralph A. Kemp, M.D.

PREFACE

This book was written to be an encouragement to myself and others who are facing the blackened face of the Grim Reaper sooner than expected. Having trekked in the Alps of Switzerland, Austria, Italy, France or Nepal annually for the last 21 years, I found myself experiencing air hunger for the first time during my last Swiss trek in Chamanna Coaz, an 8,500' snow and ice encased cliff-side mountain hut, tucked away in my bunk next to the open window as night fell. Crawling out of my sleeping bag and going outside gave me reassurance to see the distant sparkling lights of the closest village, 20 miles to the north, almost hidden in the forest. I wasn't sure if my air hunger was a physiological phenomenon with overtones of anxiety and exhaustion related to my cardiomyopathy or just exhaustion from the first days 5 hour trek to this isolated little hut. My cardiac ejection fraction, a measurement of the percentage of blood leaving the heart each time it contracts, had been stable over the last 15 years in the low 30's due to cardiomyopathy, while the normal range is 50-75. However, with this persistent air hunger was a new phenomenon, I suspected that the degree of my exhaustion was the result of an irreversible reduction of cardiac function, in spite of a normal pulse rate and rhythm. With heavy snow falling the last few miles of our trek, it now embraced the hut and the rocky trail was totally obliterated. It would be 36 hours until the trail would be sufficiently exposed to safely descend the narrow rocky cliff side and arrive to the safety of the forest, if there weren't any additional storms. During that next day of waiting out the storm for the trail to be exposed, a supply helicopter landed on the small primitive wooden helicopter pad adjacent to the